German Motorized Artillery and Panzer Artillery in World War II

Wolfgang Fleischer & Richard Eiermann

The armored artillery, thanks to their possession of offroad-capable wheeled, halftracked, and tracked vehicles and observation and communication devices, was capable of providing decisive support to the mobile combat of the tanks and armored grenadiers. This required their troops' full mastery of their weapons and equipment, foresight in planning, tactical comprehension, and sensitivity to the particular nature of armored artillery combat. Because of the fast pace of combat for armored units, it was especially important for the observers to provide constant observation and precise fire control.

German Motorized Artillery and Panzer Artillery in World War II

Wolfgang Fleischer
& Richard Eiermann

Schiffer Military History
Atglen, PA

Bibliography

H.Dv. 119/151 Shot tables for Light Howitzer 18, March 1943, Berlin 1943
H.Dv. 119/511 Shot tables for Heavy Howitzer 18, March 1943, Berlin 1943
H.Dv. 200/2 f Artillery Training Manual, Vol. 2 f, training for batteries of Heavy Howitzer 18 and 10 cm Cannon 18, April 1, 1938, Berlin 1938
H.Dv. 200/5 Artillery Training Manual, Vol. 5, Artillery command, January 26, 1937, Berlin 1937
H.Dv. 298/3a Armored Troops Training Manual, Vol. 1, Armored grenadier comand and combat, armored grenadier unit, August 5, 1944, Berlin 1944
H.Dv. 300/1 Troop Command, Vol. 1 (I-XIII), October 17, 1933, Berlin 1933
H.Dv. 300/2 Troop Command, Vol. 2 (XIV-XX11 & appendix), October 18, 1934, Berlin 1934
H.Dv. 487 Command and combat of unified weapons, June 20, 1923, Berlin 1923
D 606/7 Medium 5-ton Towing Tractor (Sd.Kfz. 6), Type BNL 8, DBL 8, June 7, 1939, Berlin 1939
D 660/1 Light 3-ton Towing Tractor Sd.Kfz. 11), T ype K1 6, October 19, 1938, Berlin 1938
D 660/6 Medium 8-ton Towing Tractor (Sd.Kfz. 7), February 6, 1939, Berlin 1939
D 684/1 Medium armored observation vehicle (Sd.Kfz. 254) on wheel/track chassis RR-7, chassis description and servicing manual, July 8, 1940, Berlin 1940
D 2020 Light Howitzer 18/2 (Sf.) on GW II, May 1, 1943, Berlin 1943
D 2051/1 Loading the Light Howitzer 18/2 (Sf.) on GW II, February 1, 1944, Berlin 1944
Art. Memo 19 Temporary Guidelines for use of the armored observation battery, November 12, 1940, Berlin 1940
Art. Memo 24 Temporary Guidelines for armored observer training and armored observation vehicle weapons, October 9, 1942, Berlin 1942
Art. Memo 25 Temporary Guidelines for use of artillery in an armored division, October 9, 1942
Vehicle Training Manual, Light Howitzer 18 II on armored SFL II, December 1942, Jüterbog 1942
Vehicle Training Manual, Heavy Howitzer 18 on armored SFL II, February 1943, Jüterbog 1943
Handbook 80/1 Guidelines for tank-artillery collaboration, September 13, 1944, Berlin 1944
Aberger, H.-D. The 5th (lt)/21st Armored Division in North Africa 1941-1943, Reutlingen 1994
Boelcke, W.A. Germany's Weapons in World War II, Frankfurt am Main 1969
Farnbacher, F. History of Artillery/Armored Artillery Regiment 103, no place, 1995
Ganns, K.H. Armored Artillery Regiment 76 1936-1945, Cologne 1962

(Bibliography cotinued on page 6)

Translated from the German by Dr. Ed Force
Book design by Joseph M. Riggio Jr.

Library of Congress Catalog Number: 2004109055

This book was originally published under the title, *Panzerfahrzeuge und Panzereinheiten der Ordnungspolizei 1936-1945* by Podzun-Pallas.

Printed in China.
ISBN: 0-7643-2095-5

Published by Schiffer Publishing Ltd.
4880 Lower Valley Road
Atglen, PA 19310
Phone: (610) 593-1777
FAX: (610) 593-2002
E-mail: info@schifferbooks.com.
Visit our web site at: www.schifferbooks.com
Please write for a free catalog.
This book may be purchased from the publisher.
Please include $3.95 postage.
Try your bookstore first.
In Europe, Schiffer books are distributed by:
Bushwood Books
6 Marksbury Ave.
Kew Gardens
Surrey TW9 4JF
England
Phone: 44 (0)208 392-8585
FAX: 44 (0)208 392-9876
E-mail: info@bushwoodbooks.co.uk.
Free postage in the UK. Europe: air mail at cost.
Try your bookstore first.

CONTENTS

The origins of motorized artillery in the Reichswehr.

(cotinued from page 4)

Guderian, H. Achtung - Tanks!, Stuttgart, no year
“” Memoirs of a Soldier, Stuttgart 1986
Heigl, F. Pocket Bok of Tanks, Munich 1926
“” Pocket Book of Tanks, Complete 1927, Munich 1927
“” Pocket Book of Tanks, 1930 edition, Munich 1930
Kruse, K. Artillery Advisor on the Battlefield, Munich 1943
Kurtzinski, M.J. Tactics of Fast Units, Potsdam 1935
Plato, D.A. von History of the 5th Armored Division 1938-1945, Regensburg, 1978
Ritgen, H. History of the Armored Training Divivion in the West 1944-45, Stuttgart 1979
Saucken, D. von 4th Armored Division, Part II May 1943-May 1945, no place, 19691 [sic]
Scheibert, H. The Ghost Division - A German Armored Division (7th) in World War II, Friedberg, no date
Senger und Etterlin, F.M. von The German Guns 1939-1945, Munich 1960
“” “” The 24th Armored Division, ex-1st Cavalry Division, Neckargmünd 1962
“” “” The German Tanks 1926-1945, Munich 1968
Spaeter, H. The History of the Armored Corps GD, Vol. II, Bielefeld, no year
Spielberger, W.J. The German Panzer III and IV and their variants 1935-1945, Munich 1968
“” Panzer I and II and their variants, Stuttgart 1984
“” Panzer IV and its variants, Stuttgart 1984
Stäber, H.J. The Iron Fist, photos and chronicles of the 17th SS Armored Grenadier Division “Götz von Berlichingen,” Neckargmünd 1966
Stoves, R. The 1st Armored Division 1935-1945, Dorheim, no year
Tieke, W. The Firestorm of the Last War Years. Osnabrück 1975
Newspapers and Magazines: Artilleristische Rundschau, Militärwochenblatt, Militärwissenschaftliche Rundschau, Wehrtechnische Monatshefte

Photo Credits
Almstedt (8), Bischof (4), Bräuer (1), Eiermann (39), Faustka (3), Federal Archives (3), Fleischer (175), Fuchs (2), Heiss (1), Hoppe (20), Jülch (4), Mack (1), Peeters (1), Wetzig (6), Wiese (8), WTS (5).

FOREWORD

The armored artillery developed from the motorized artillery of the armored divisions, the rifle divisions (mot.), and the light divisions of the German Army. The concept of armored artillery was first used during the 1937 autumn maneuvers. It was introduced in March 1942 as the official designation of the most mobile part of the field artillery. Its origins go back farther, to World War I, and are closely linked with the development of theoretical and practical concepts of the use of armored weapons in the twenties and thirties. The idea of using tanks as a new means of battle in warfare, within the parameters of fast, mobile, and independently acting operative armored groups, gained more and more adherents in those times. Among them was Oberstleutnant Heinz Guderian, who rose to the rank of Inspector General of Armored Troops during World War II. Following the British model, he foresaw in the armored divisions not only tank units, but also motorized troops with all other weapons. These included riflemen, the artillery, intelligence troops, engineers, and supply units. For the artillery in particular, with its heavy and sensitive guns, various equipment, and extensive supply lines, numerous new technical and tactical demands developed out of the basic concept that "armored units...[are] less a means of penetration than the means of maneuvering and mobility...." In World War I, much deprived of their mobility, they had functioned, offensively and defensively, primarily as prepared firing positions with long-term destructive fire, and had negatively influenced the course of combat action. Now one had to part from these concepts. In the mid-thirties, with the establishment of motorized artillery regiments in the armored divisions and other units with modern equipment, it was not just the artillerymen's technical firing capability that was required.
The creation of technical, tactical, and organizational prerequisites for artillery combat conduct based on mobile war required sensitivity and an understanding of the essential characteristics of armored combat. The task of the armored artillery was to bring the firepower of their guns, directed according to concepts of artillery use, to support tank and armored grenadier units on the battlefield. Their possession of offroad-capable towing tractors made possible a mobility comparable to that of the tanks. But only in 1942-43, with the reequipping of part of the armored artillery with light self-propelled gun mounts and armored scout cars, was a link forged between the artillery components with high tactical mobility and armor protection. Only at this point did the technical-tactical parameters of these weapons come into agreement with the concept of armored artillery introduced in 1942. Armored howitzer units were the essential artillery of the armored battle groups, composed of tanks, armored grenadiers, and engineers in the last two war years. It was their task in the mobile defensive combat to stabilize their own fronts that had been shaken by the attacks of numerically superior enemy mechanized and armored units. [p. 8] Technical and tactical experiences were evaluated by Germany's enemies and influenced the buildup of comparable formations in their forces. After World War II the development of ABC weapons hastened the development of the armored artillery. Everywhere they became components of mechanized and armored units.
The authors thank Oberst a.D. Gerhard Elser of Oldenburg and Frau Sonja Wetzig of Dresden.

Freital, Autumn 2000

Wolfgang Fleischer, Richard Eiermann

Action during a display of motorized artillery on a Reich Party Day of the NSDAP in Nuremberg. On such occasions special maneuver cartridges were fired.

I. THE TWENTIES: THE FIRST MOTORIZED FIELD ARTILLERY

In the search for the origins of motorized and armored artillery in the German Army, several basic lines of development of military technology and tactics must be considered. They go back to World War I and include:

1. The introduction of motor tractors for the artillery

The German Army was able to gather experience in the prewar era. Usable technical solutions were found only during the war, after the upgrading of artillery material, which had become necessary, exceeded the most determined horsedrawn weights. It was soon seen that the requirements for an artillery towing tractor could be met only by a vehicle with four wheel drive. Only this guaranteed the full utilization of the vehicle's high weight by dividing it among four driven wheels. In this respect, the Krupp-Daimler artillery tractor proved itself best during the war, when it was used to tow the heavy 15-cm Cannon 16. Wheeled tractors had numerous uses, enabling high speeds on roads and firm paths, as well as comparable off-road terrain. With their heavy ground pressure, they could not meet their requirements on soft ground. Tracked tractors like the A 7 V off-road type, which had been used in small numbers, did not have this disadvantage. Their disadvantages were their steering and suspension. Then too, the tracks were very stressed under high-speed road transit. For this reason, artillery tractors with wheel-track running gear were favored after World War I. Their high road speeds attracted attention. The designing of such vehicles was not brought to a conclusion in the twenties.

In Germany, a series of basic investigations had taken place at the beginning of the thirties; their goal was the development of suitable tractors for the artillery. The Army Weapons Office did not want to rely on stock vehicles, the advantages of which consisted only of lower production costs.

They had to meet the military requirements both on and off roads. These investigations resulted in a definition of the characteristics of such tractors. They were to be halftrack vehicles, with padded and lubricated steel steering tracks and drive wheels at the front. They would attain fairly fast road speeds with little power output, but likewise be able to put the necessary towing power on the ground when off the road. The necessary on-road sensitivity in the steering could not be achieved with the Cletrac steering gear. This was assured by the front wheels, which allowed minor directional correction (to 15%) when taking gentle curves at high speeds, while sharper curves could be taken with additional use of the steering gear. In April 1933 the Krauss-Maffei firm displayed the prototype of the first Kmz 85 halftrack towing tractor to the Inspector of Motor Vehicles, General Lutz. It already included the box tracked running gear developed by Oberbaurat Kniepkamp. On May 28, 1934, Krauss-Maffei became the

A Krupp-Daimler KD 1 towing tractor with all wheel drive and iron tires is towing the barrel wagon of the heavy 15 cm Cannon 16 (weighing 8290 kg). At the end of World War I, motorized battalions of three batteries had been established in the foot artillery of the German Army, using this type of gun. They were used with the long-distance battle groups of the army corps.

A Lanz artillery tractor tows a wheeled mount for the 17 cm L/40 rapid-fire cannon. The ponderous gun was in use by the Navy. The mount of the bed wagon alone weighed more than 12,000 kg. The tractor had rear wheel drive and was powered by an 80 to 100 HP motor. This one was photographed in 1917.

general contractor for the production of the 8-ton towing tractor, which went into series production in the same year with the designation KM m 8. In all, there were six different sizes of halftrack tractors, of which the 3-, 5-, 8-, and 12-ton types were especially important for the artillery.

Testing of the full-tracked tractor made by the Gesellschaft für Frachttransport (Gefrat) at the end of the twenties showed again the disadvantages of this type of vehicle already known from World War I.

During World War I, small numbers of A7V offroad vehicles were used. The vehicle was designed as a gun or ammunition tractor for a load of 10,000 kg—15,000 kg with a trailer—and was used in the Army's tracked-vehicle columns. The powerplants were two 100 HP carbureted motors that had to be engaged together for straight-ahead movement. For curves, one motor was declutched.

A motorized battery of Artillery Regiment 5 is seen on parade on the Cathedral Square in Ulm, on the Danube. The tractor for the 10.5 cm light Howitzer 16 was the Linke-Hofmann tractor, fitted with a Diesel engine and capable of speeds up to 12 kph.

The Krupp-Daimler KD 1 tractor saw service in World War I as an artillery tractor with iron tires. As of 1924 the Daimler-Benz factory in Berlin-Marienfelde delivered this vehicle to the Reichswehr with hard rubber tires. They improved the performance of the all wheel tractor with its 100 HP gasoline engine.

2. The first self-propelled artillery gun mounts

Between July and September 1918, 48 "Gun Carrier Mk I" vehicles with 152.4 mm cannons were built for the British Tank Corps.

If one looks at the motorized guns used in Germany, one sees that these vehicles were the first, and in this case the first armored, self-propelled gun mounts of the Artillery. It was their task to follow the tanks into shell-crater terrain, so as to be able to afford them fire support if needed. An idea that probably originated on the battlefield of Cambrai in November 1917, when the attacking British tanks had tried to put down the German defenses in laborious struggles far from their own lines, was surely far ahead of its time. Thus, it was not by chance that some of these vehicles were used by the engineer troops as "supply carriers." The design, comparable to the cannon transporter, was adopted after World War I by, among others, Italy, France, and Russia.

Another type of self-propelled gun was the already noted truck gun. This was the anti-balloon gun, which was mounted on trucks for the purpose of attacking aircraft. It proved its superiority during World War I, particularly in its high operative and tactical mobility, which allowed artillery firepower†to be moved quickly to threatened sectors of the front. In the German Army this weapon gained great significance, especially in antitank action. The blend of firepower and mobility was developed further for the Reichswehr after the war. The artillery regiments could each include a battery of self-propelled guns. They found use as infantry escort or assault guns, and as a highly mobile artillery reserve, especially in fighting off tank attacks. They were no longer usable as anti-aircraft guns. According to information from the Allied victors, their effective range of elevation was limited to 30 degrees, thus their aiming for firing on air targets was ruined. A truck gun weighed 8.9 tons and could travel at 12 to 20 kph, depending on its tires. With the 7.7 cm gun, targets up to 7500 meters away could be reached with the explosive shell with contact fuze.

The Krupp-Daimler or Rheinmetall/Erhardt Gun Vehicle 14 was one of the German Army's first self-propelled gun mounts in World War I. It carried a 7.7 cm anti-aircraft gun with a range of 7800 meters, or an elevation of 4250 meters. In addition to anti-aircraft use, it was of special importance in antitank action.

Between 1924 and 1930, 49 KD 1 gun trucks (Sd.Kfz. 1) with 7.7 cm anti-aircraft guns of the 1911 or 1914 model were built for the Reichswehr. The guns were no longer suitable for anti-aircraft use, but constituted a very mobile reinforcement of the field artillery of the Reichswehr. The unarmored vehicle weighed 11,240 kg and could attain a speed of 35 kph.

The basic structure of a motorized battery as of 1928 had it equipped with four truck-mounted guns on the improved Type 19 truck, four ammunition vehicles, one Type 19 scout car, and two artillery tractors. Note that it also included 13 saddle and draft horses, as well as four horsedrawn wagons. The Army Weapons Office of the Reichswehr requested, in a communication dated May 24, 1928, the provision of financial means to provide twelve 7.5 cm barrels for the truck guns in the coming year. For the future army of 16 divisions there was a basic need of 112 gun barrels. The replacement of 7.7 with 7.5 cm barrels was completed in 1932. Truck-mounted guns were supposed to be used in attacks primarily in overtaking and pursuit. If need be, the reconnaissance units of the army artillery could be strengthened with this mobile artillery system. In defensive operations their most important tasks included antitank action. It was customary to hold back the truck-mounted guns as reserves and then send them against the attackers.

Despite the limited means available, self-propelled gun mounts continued to play a role in the Reichswehr's development program. A successor model to the truck gun may have been considered, for in new developments the capability for antitank use was always an important part of military requirements. As early as 1927 the Rheinmetall-Borsig GmbH firm had exhibited the heavy version of the WD tractor with a 7.7 cm gun. This group of vehicles also included the Krupp tracked vehicle (LSK) and the Horch halftrack. A 7.7 cm 96/16 cannon, which was intended to be the armament for both. In a discussion notice of the Army Weapons Office/Weapon Testing VI dated February 14, 1930, it was stated for both vehicles:

"The development of the Krupp tracked vehicle and the Horch halftrack must be continued, since it has already made much progress, and it has not been determined whether the chassis of the light tractor is suited to this purpose."

Several armies repeatedly stressed that the weapon carriers for truck-mounted guns must not be too expensive, for their production would otherwise be unrealistic.

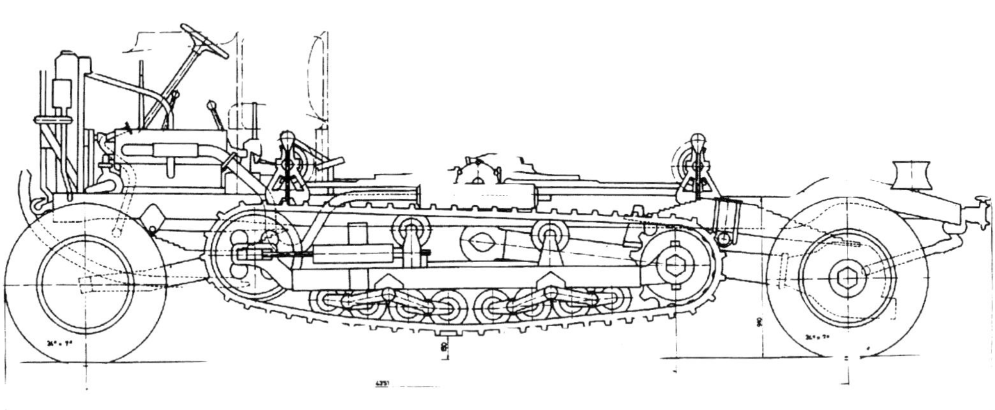

The Maffei firm developed this wheeled/tracked tractor in 1930. Only prototypes were built and tested.

The project ended with the building and testing of prototypes. This was also true of the Maffei firm's halftrack tractor with a 7.7 anti-balloon gun, dating from 1930.

As a result of plans made by the Reichswehr's weapons office, 120 gun barrels were replaced with 7.5 cm types between 1930 and 1932, including the barrels of all the Type 14 truck-mounted guns. This was accompanied by a designation change: the 7.7 cm Cannon 16 was from then on called the 7.5 cm Cannon 16 n.A. (new version). It was used by the Army's artillery regiments.

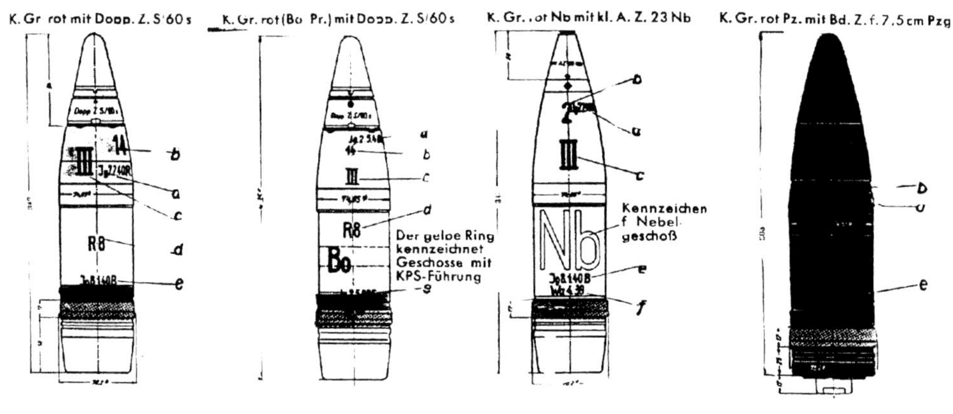

The ammunition for the 7.5 cm Cannon n.A. With the red cannon shell weighing 5.83 kg, either the contact fuze 23 v. (0.15) or the double fuze S/60 could be used, and ranges up to 12875 meters were attainable. For antitank use the 7.5 cm red antitank cannon shell was available. At a range of 500 meters it had a penetrating power of 61 mm of steel armor plate.

3. Updating Artillery Weapons

According to the Treaty of Versailles, which went into effect on January 10, 1920, the artillery armament of the Reichswehr was limited to 204 96/16 and 16 cannons, 84 light howitzers, 22 fixed guns, and 16 anti-aircraft guns. These were all models from World War I times. A large number of available artillery weapons were scrapped or had to be handed over to the Entente or associated countries. A side effect of this disarmament, compelled by the powers that won World War I, was that decisions about future rearmament could be made freely without having to take into

To move the 7.5 cm Cannon 16 n.A., which weighed 1524 kg, it had to be loaded onto the Trailer 1 (1 axle) for light loads (Sd.Anh. 3). The empty trailer weighed 850 kg.

This trailer, designated Sd.Anh. 1, was classified as a single-axle trailer for light and medium guns, and was already being tested in 1929.

This 10.5 cm Light Howitzer 16 is†loaded on a two-axle special trailer that†was towed in a parade in the capital city of Berlin by a KM 7a medium towing tractor. In firing position the gun weighed 1450 kg.

account the mass of military technology that was available in great quantities but was outmoded. In the specialist press, the question of how the field artillery of the future army should appear was discussed all the more vigorously.

Because of the ban on the development and production of modern weapons and equipment the Reichswehr leadership had to proceed very cautiously. In this respect, a comment of December 28, 1935, that the author of the book "The Equipment of the Light Artillery Before, In and After the World War," retired Generalleutnant Alfred Muther, added to one of his books is very significant:

"Since it is not wanted that the attention of more extensive circles, particularly outside the country, be directed to this book, it is requested that discussions in journals, etc., be avoided...."

The experience gained in the war can be summed up as follows: first, a greater shot range was required; and second, increased effect of the individual shot. Light howitzers and cannons were supposed to be present in the divisions at ratios of 1:1 or 2:1. The 10.5 cm caliber applied to both guns and was regarded as very promising. A 7.5 cm shell was only half as heavy as one of 10.5 cm

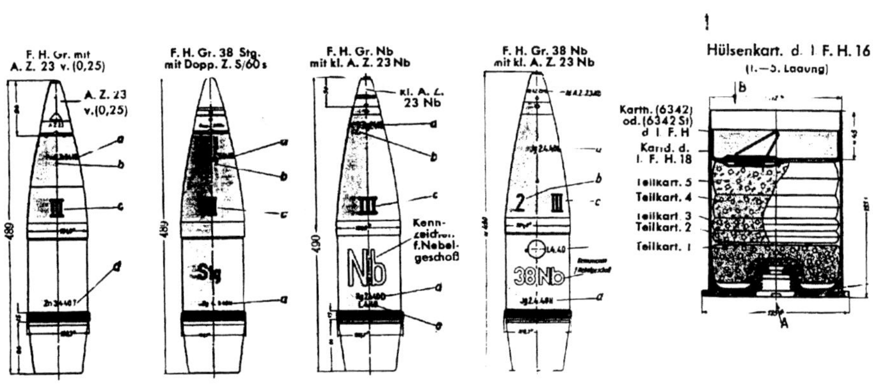

The ammunition for the 10.5 cm Light Howitzer 16. For the 14.81 kg 38 stg howitzer shell a range of 9225 meters could be attained with the fifth charge.

In the spring of 1935 the first 10.5 cm Light Howitzer 18s, made for motorized towing, were already being tested by the troops. On the march the gun weighed over 2000 kg, in firing position 1925 kg.

The usual towing tractor for the 10.5 cm Light Howitzer 18 was the 3-ton light tractor (Sd.Kfz. 11). This vehicle could attain a speed of 52.5 kph.

More rarely, the 5-ton medium tractor (Sd.Kfz. 6) was used to tow the 10.5 cm Light Howitzer 18 (motor-towed). In its final BN9 version it used a 115 HP Maybach motor that allowed speeds up to 50 kph.

The 15 cm Heavy Howitzer 18 (motor-towed) was found before the war only to the extent of one unit in the artillery regiments of the motorized infantry divisions, and in a few independent heavy units. The one exception was the 2nd Armored Division. Its motorized artillery regiment had one heavy and one light unit.

Demonstrating a 15 cm Heavy Howitzer 18 (motor-towed) at the Nazi Party Day in Nuernberg. Its weight in firing position was stated as 5512 kg. On the march it weighed 6304 kg.

caliber. Thus the barrel, to be able to deliver a comparable weight to the target, had to be stressed twice as often. The author of the article†"Cannon and Howitzer" in Militärwochenblatt No. 7, 1924, Hauptmann Fritz Lindemann, opposed this argument, saying that the greater range of the cannon had to be rated more highly. Only a third of a division's artillery should consist of howitzers. The retired Oberst Baron von Weitershausen also advocated mixed guns, such as had been customary in the German Army at the end of World War I. An anonymous author wrote in the Militärwochenblatt on the subject of "tactical artillery thoughts in the recent and future" in 1925:

"In choosing between cannons and howitzers it must be borne in mind that the cannon is technically better suited for observed fire on visible targets, likewise pinpoint targets like tanks.... On the other hand, suitable cannon positions are rare. Their location requires much time."

With its seventh charge the 15 cm Heavy Howitzer 18 could attain a range of 13,325 meters. The rate of fire was listed as four shots per minute.

A decision in favor of the 10.5 cm light and 15 cm heavy howitzers was made in the latter half of the twenties. A light cannon was rejected; only a heavy 10 cm cannon was still being developed. Firing positions for howitzers were easier to find, which shortened the positioning and the time needed to open fire. Howitzers, with their variable trajectories, offered better possible effect against hidden targets. Their larger shells were a further advantage. Their disadvantages, including their lesser range and very limited ability to fight armored targets, were regarded as having to be taken in the bargain.

In the Army Weapons Office's priority list of June 1, 1927, the development of the 10.5 cm light howitzer had been advanced. The developmental firm wasRheinmetall-Borsig GmbH. The new design of the 15 cm heavy howitzer had already been advanced by the Artillery Testing Commission in 1917. Development could be undertaken by the F. Krupp AG and Rheinmetall-Borsig GmbH only in the latter half of the twenties. Officially the 15 cm heavy howitzer and the light howitzer were introduced in 1935. The light howitzer was the uniform gun of the field artillery; a light cannon was rejected. Another new design was the 10 cm heavy cannon, likewise introduced in 1935. All three guns bore the model number 18 and were built for horse-drawn or motorized towing. Thus, important technical prerequisites existed for the field artillery of the German Army, typified by the appearance of the motorized and armored artllery.

The 8-ton medium tractor (Sd.Kfz, 7) was used to tow the 15 cm Heavy Howitzer 18. This picture shows the first production model (KM m 8), which was built by the Krauss Maffei firm in 1934-35. The 6-cylinder Maybach motor of this vehicle type produced 115 HP amd allowed a top speed of 50 kph. It could tow loads up to 8000 kg.

II. THE THIRTIES
MOTORIZED ARTILLERY
FOR LARGE ARMORED UNITS

The fascination that the vision of mechanized war in the future inspired in the twenties and thirties is seen in the description of a show by the British Tank Corps in Camberley, written by the well-known military journalist B. H. Liddell Hart:

"A battery of self-propelled 18-pound guns took up a position to our left. Then a number of small one- and two-man tanks appeared and hastened forward, while from a thicket behind us the muzzle flash of a thick row of positioned Vickers tanks was seen; suddenly they emerged from the bushes and stormed forward in a ferocious attack, more fearful to see than any cavalry attack, with resounding guns and clattering machine guns...."

Liddell Hart had drawn a picture of a future battle, defined by armored troops and their collaboration with other weapons, especially the artillery. This resulted in special requirements for these weapons. The outlook on this had undergone further development in the first half of the thirties. In his 1937 book "Achtung - Panzer!" Guderian summed it up:

"The attack (of the tanks)...required...support by the artillery. The artillery's tasks are holding open those targets and areas of land that afford space for the tank attack, such as villages, woods, steep slopes, water and swamp areas, holding down or blinding suspected observation posts and positions of defensive weapons, destroying recognized targets that could affect the tank attack.... Horsedrawn artillery certainly cannot follow a successful tank attack; it is hard enough for guns moved by tractors. Thus the armored troops want and need accompanying artillery that is so mobile and protected that it is capable of following the tank attack directly. In addition to its special means of mobility, this artillery needs certain practice and thus certain training in cooperating with tanks. Its direction is more difficult than that of the infantry divisions' artillery, for the time of its effectiveness is shorter and its targets more changing.

A tank attack does not require any unified, previously determined necessary fire, any artillery preparation by 'softening up' positions; rather it requires a nimble, quick and sure-shooting artillery...."

These are characteristic technical and tactical requirements for the artillery in the armored divisions. Guderian's wishes for an artillery on armored self-propelled mounts, or, as Walther Nehring described it in 1935, "Special combat vehicles as armored artillery carriers (tank-accompanying artillery)," were not yet adopted at that time. Corresponding developments of the twenties did not go beyond the testing stage. Half a decade later Germany lacked the needed developmental and production facilities. For these reasons the armored troops had to be satisfied at first with artillery made mobile by being towed by motor vehicles, meaning halftrack towing tractors.

In 1938-39 the motor vehicle testing arm of the Army Weapons Office tested the 3-ton HL kl 5 light towing tractor (Sd.Kfz. 11). The improved HL kl 6 version was built in large numbers until 1944. It was the most important means of towing the 10.5 cm Light Howitzer 19 (motor-towed).

Here the HL kl 5 light 3-ton towing tractor (Sd.Kfz. 11) is seen with two special (one-axle) trailers during a show on the grounds of the Army Test Center in Kummersdorf.

This KM m 8 8-ton medium towing tractor (Sd.Kfz. 7) pulls a 15 cm Howitzer 18 (motor-towed). The tractor and gun together weighed more than 17 tons.

Eight-ton medium towing tractors of the KM 9 and 10 types (Sd.Kfz. 7) were built by Krauss-Maffei in 1936 and 1937. Among their typical external identifying marks are short track running gear and strongly arched front fenders. Using a 130-to-140 HP six-cylinder Maybach engine improved their performance. They were seldom seen towing the 10.5 cm Light Howitzer 18 (above). More typically they were used by the motorized artillery to tow the 15 cm Heavy Howitzer 18.

A 15 cm Heavy Howitzer 18 (motor-towed) in firing position. The cost of building such a gun decreased from 50,000 to 44,000 Reichsmark in 1938.

The 8-ton medium tractor (Sd.Kfz. 7) was tested under combat conditions in the Spanish Civil War (1936-1939) by work commands of the Army Weapons Office (Wa Prüf IV and VI). The picture shows a KM m 8 tractor.

The chassis of the KM m 11 8-ton medium towing tractor (Sd.Kfz. 7)

Effective October 15, 1935, the first three armored divisions of the Army were established. Their war structure included a motorized artillery regiment with two sections of three batteries each. The establishment of the motorized artillery units was already in full swing at that time, and sometimes completed. An interesting view of those changing times was afforded at the end of the thirties by a brief account of the history of the 1st Unit of Artillery Regiment (mot.) 73. It belonged to the 1st Armored Division (Weimar). On November 1, 1934, a motorized light artillery unit was assembled out of parts of the IV. Unit of Artillery Regiment 3 at the Ohrdruf Troop Training Camp. It was designated the Ohrdruf Light Artillery Unit. It set the pattern for the establishment of motorized Artillery Regiments 73, 74, and 75 in 1936.

On the day when the Ohrdruf Light Artillery Unit was establishedit had a total of six old, stock motor vehicles, which were used for driving school purposes. For lack of vehicles, the recruits' training was done on foot at first. In January 1935 the unit received four 10.5 cm Light Howitzer 16 and four agricultural tractors (top speed 12 kph). In the following weeks box vans, guns, motorcycles, and the first towing tractors arrived. In April 1935 the unit moved to the Ohrdruf troop training center for training. At this time the batteries each had four 10.5 cm Light Howitzer 16 guns. To be able to use them in the motorized artillery they were loaded onto 1-axle special trailers for light loads (Sd.Anh.3). The guns had to be unloaded to be fired, which was difficult and time-consuming, especially on soft ground. At the end of April 1935 two Army batteries were given the order to test a newly designed gun (the 10.5 cm Light Howitzer 18) as to its utility in the field, and to gather experience with it. One of these batteries was the 1st of

In addition to towing tractors, the motorized artillery received numerous other motor vehicles. The medium offroad-capable truck with closed body, doors, and windows (Kfz. 72) existed in 15 different versions. In the motorized artillery it was used as, among other things, sound evaluation and telephone trucks.

In the motor pools of the supply trains there were, among others, light offroad-capable 1.5-ton Marcedes-Benz G3 a trucks, used as field kitchens. In this version the kitchen stove is aboard.

the Ohrdruf Light Artillery Unit. By summer's end the experience report on this gun could be submitted. It was positive; the 10.5 cm Light Howitzer 18 was, as already noted, accepted for introduction into the light artillery units of the Army. In the ensuing winter, training of recruits on the new gun could be commenced.

In the summer months of 1935, some batteries of the Ohrdruf Light Artillery Unit, along with motorized rifle battalions, carried out training exercises at various training centers. The high point was the testing of the armored troops at the Munster Troop Training Center in August 1935.

At the beginning of October 1935 the unit moved into the newly erected barracks at Weimar. On November 6, 1936, Artillery Regiment (mot.) 73 was established, with its I. Unit in Weimar and II. Unit in Erfurt. The regimental staff followed on April 1, 1937. This was the development of the motorized artillery of the Army's armored divisions in the mid-thirties, which could only be portrayed on the basis of the I. Unit, Artillery Regiment (mot.) 73 as an example. Also, on October 6, 1936, Artillery Regiments (mot.) 74 and 75 were established; they belonged to the 2nd and 3rd Armored Divisions. As of October 15, 1935, the 2nd Cavalry Division also had a light motorized artillery unit, which was formed from Mounted Artillery Unit 3. In the establishment of light divisions, which was done on the basis of the Army cavalry divisions in 1938, an alternative to the armored divisions was seen. In the forefront of the establishment of these units were discussions about various structural models for the motorized artillery. From the 8th Unit of the Army General Staff came the suggestion in June 1936 to assign to the light divisions, besides a heavy motorized artillery unit, a light motorized artillery unit in each of the two cavalry rifle regiments. This suggestion resembled a setup used by the Red Army and had been publicized by M. J. Kurtzinski in the book "Taktik schneller Verbände" (German translation published in

Potsdam in 1935). Kurtzinski described in detail the mechanized brigade of the Russian cavalry, which could have a total of 18 SU-12 self-propelled guns in its three regiments. They were the 76.2 mm 1927 regimental cannon on offroad-capable GAZ-AAA (6x4) trucks. In Germany a different course was taken; the four light divisions gained motorized artillery regiments with two light units. Also included in the plans of the mid-thirties were armored brigades, which were to function as Army troops according to the concepts of the Army General Staff. Here the inclusion of a motorized artillery unit was planned, with its primary task being the attacking of enemy antitank weapons, which called for special training in collaboration with tanks. This was done in the establishment of the 4th and 6th Tank Brigades (Stuttgart and Paderborn). The former was formed in 1939 in the Kempf Armored Division, and later incorporated into the 10th Armored Division. The independent Tank Brigade 6 staff was disbanded in 1939.

When the German Army began to motorize the artillery of the light and armored division, the experience from long years of horsedrawn batteries was used as much as possible. Battery troop, intelligence unit, combat battery, two ammunition units, and supply trains were structured similarly. This enabled the addition of personnel, some of whom came from the horsedrawn artillery units.

Many of these officers and NCOs had to obtain a driver's license first. Short courses provided their radio training and put it on a new basis—corresponding to the command and fire control of an armored division. The performance of motorized equipment allowed top speeds of almost 50 kph, and also let the batteries depart far from the marching order to get ready to fire. The use of the artillery had to be suited to whatever use was made of tanks. The focal point of their

As a commaander's vehicle in the motorized artillery, the Wanderer W 11 (Kfz.12) medium offroad personnel vehicle was used, as were other types of vehicles. Between 1929 and 1932 2844 of them were delivered.

Demonstrations of the 10 cm Heavy Cannon 18 were included in Reich Party Day events in Nuremberg. The motor-towed version, which was used by the motorized artillery, weighed 5,642 kg in firing position. In the background a 15cm Heavy Cannon 16 (motor-towed) can be seen.

combat activity was the task of providing particular fire cover for their own tank forces. On command, the tank attack had to be covered by gunfire directed by the artillery observers. Since the artillery was motorized but not armored, it could not follow right after the tank attack. Yet as early as 1937, the concept of "armored artillery" first appeared on the occasion of firing practice with light howitzers in an armored division (see Artilleristische Rundschau, Vol. 10, 1937, pp. 523ff.).

In 1937-38 the temporary artillery tractors, including Linke-Hofmann tracked farm tractors and Type MSZ 201 towing tractors (the Reichswehr had bought 24 of them in 1931), were replaced by the 3-, 5-, and 8-ton classes. In 1936 the Hanse-Lloyd-Goliath AG of Bremen began to produce the 3-ton light towing tractor (Sd.Kfz.11), used primarily to tow the 10.5 Light Howitzer 18. In marching trim the gun weighed 3490 kg. The 5-ton medium towing tractor (Sd.Kfz.6/1) made by the Büssing-NAG firm in Berlin-Oberschöneweide appeared in much smaller numbers in the light artillery units. The first vehicles were delivered in 1934.

For the 15 cm Heavy Howitzer 18, which still weighed a massive 6304 kg in marching trim, the 8-ton medium towing tractor (Sd.Kfz.7) was used. Pre-production vehicles of type KM 7 had been assembled at the Krauss-Maffei works in Munich in October 1933. This company alone turned out 380 of the first production model (KM m 8), plus 120 of its successor, the KM m 9. The 8-ton medium towing tractor was also used by the 10 cm cannon batteries of the motorized heavy artillery units to tow the 10 cm Heavy Cannon 18, which weighed 6434 kg in marching trim. The halftrack towing tractors were among the most typical vehicles of the German Army; in the prewar years they set the scene when motorized units were seen on maneuvers or

Parts of a light howitzer battery (mot.) are unloading their guns. The towing vehicles are Type HL kl 6 (Sd.Kfz.11), and the guns are 10.5 cm Light Howitzer 18 (motor-towed).

These 8-ton KM m 11 medium towing tractors (Sd.Kfz.7), towing 15 cm Heavy Howitzer 18 (motor-towed) guns, are about to march out into the field.

These 10 cm Heavy Cannon 18 are ready to march, towed by 3-ton medium offroad-capable (6 x 4) truck—a solution that was used at the time for lack of medium towing tractors.

The allowable gross weight of the 8-ton KM m 11 medium towing tractor (Sd.Kfz.7) was stated as 11,550 kg.

in parades, and they proved themselves in all theaters of war during World War II. Their high performance in mobile warfare remains undenied, though it was attained with a technically complex design. High standards were demanded for their maintenance and servicing. In the war, the Army Weapons Office worked on successor models of simpler design. Once again a question arises in this respect: why were the armored divisions not already equipped with armored self-propelled gun mounts before the war? Conceptional and technical preliminary work on such vehicles had been done at the end of the twenties. Answering this question does not become any easier when one compares the costs of motorized artillery and artillery on self-propelled mounts. A 10.5 cm Light Howitzer 18 cost 32,000 Reichsmark in 1936, and the 3-ton towing tractor for it (Sd.Kfz.11) cost 22,000 RM. For a 15 cm Heavy Howitzer 18 the cost was 50,000 RM, and a medium 8-ton towing tractor cost 36,000 RM. In all, that added up to 54,000 to 86,000 RM for a motorized gun. Since exact production costs for the Gun Car II and III/IV built from 1943 on cannot be obtained, realistic estimates based on comparable tanks amount to 45,000 RM for the 10.5 Light Howitzer 18/2 on Panzerkampfwagen II chassis (Sd.Kfz. 124), and 90,000 RM for the 15 cm Heavy Howitzer 18/1 on Gun Car III/IV (Sd.Kfz.165).The comparison shows small difference in the production costs, a result that is of little help in answering the original question. Theoretical requirements for artillery on self-propelled mounts had already been discussed in all their ramifications by theoreticians of tank warfare—including Guderian and Nehring—before the war. The fact that they could not gain an audience can be explained by the lack of understanding of some contemporaries in high military command positions—but this alone is not sufficient as a reason. A listing of the disadvantages of the armored self-propelled mounts (which will be given in detail elsewhere) is not convincing, either. It is clear that their production would have required the tank-building industry to work at capacity. For if there were, in the latter half of the thirties, a period of hectic armament, clear focal points for their manufacture would have involved the construction of tanks. On November 30, 1938, the Army had five armored divisions, with their artillery regiments (mot.) composed of two light units of three batteries (in all, twelve 10.5 cm Light Howitzer 18). The only exception at that time was the 2nd Armored Division.

Its Artillery Regiment (mot.) 74 had a light and a heavy unit. The motorized artillery regiments in the light divisions were divided into two light units, each with twelve 10.5 cm Light Howitzer 18 guns. At this time only the motorized infantry divisions had stronger

Pictures from the first campaigns: here the light 3-ton HL kl 6 Towing Tractor (Sd.Kfz.11) is seen on the march with the 10.5 cm Light Howitzer 18.

This picture was taken during the 1940 French campaign. The tactical emblem on the 5-ton BN 9 Medium Towing Tractor (Sd.Kfz. 6) indicates that tractor and gun belonged to a 1st battery of Light Howitzer 18 (mot.) guns of the I. (light) unit of an artillery regiment of an armored division.

This 8-ton KM m 11 Medium, Towing Tractor (Sd.Kfz.7) and 15 cm Heavy Howitzer 18 (mot.) belonged to the 7th battery of the III. (heavy) unit of an artillery regiment of a motorized infantry or armored division.

For the 10 cm Heavy Cannon 18 too, the customary tractor was the 8-ton medium towing tractor (Sd.Kfz.7). In the III. (heavy) unit of the motorized artillery regiments, which first appeared in the armored divisions in 1940, there was a battery with four guns of this type.

Loading drill with a 5-ton BN 9 Medium Towing Tractor (Sd.Kfz.6). The artillery version of this vehicle weighed some 7500 kg empty, 8900 kg loaded. Thus, it belonged to Loading Class Ia.

artillery, and were comparable on the basis of their artillery firepower with the infantry divisions of the first to fourth waves of establishment. In the three light units there were, in all, 36 10.5 cm Light Howitzer 18 guns, and twelve 15 cm v Heavy Howitzer 18 in the heavy unit. There was also a motorized observation unit.

The amount of ammunition that could be fired by a motorized artillery regiment during one minute of firing was 2275.2 kg, considerably lower than that of an artillery regiment in an infantry division (= 5500.8 kg). That was too little for the armored divisions. A comparison of the artillery firepower had become unignorable because of the qualitative and quantitative strengthening of antitank defense in the latter half of the thirties. Artillery in motorized and armored divisions meant a combination of high firepower and great mobility.

The characteristics of combat were determined by the use of tanks. It was important to adapt to constantly changing combat situations, not to lose orientation, and not let contact with the tank groups be broken. Great distances had to be overcome within short times, and recognized targets fought quickly and precisely. Under these conditions the observation of the target area and the artillery's fire control were of particular significance. Both had to take place up front where the tanks were. Thus, the motorized artillery was richly equipped with means of observation and communication. Whoever led from the front was, like the tanks, exposed to the direct fire of the enemy's defensive weapons. The loss of advanced observers made the artillery blind—a recognition that led to the request for armored scout cars.

Suitable vehicles were designed on the basis of the armored troop transporters of the

Driving training in a heavy unit of the motorized artillery.

motorized rifle units, but were no longer available when the war began. Thus, in the motorized artillery regiments various makeshift solutions were utilized. In Artillery Regiment (mot.) 75 of the 3rd Armored Division, each battery received two Armored Command Car I (Sd.Kfz.265), Type B as armored scout cars. In the chronicles of Artillery Regiment (mot.) 103 (4th Armored Division) the receipt of several Panzerkampfwagen I (Sd.Kfz.101) in the spring of 1939 was reported; they served as substitutes for lacking armored scout cars. The worn-out vehicles could be kept in running order only with much trouble. In addition, they were needed at frist for the training of tank drivers, and later Panzerkampfwagen II (Sd.Kfz. 121) were added.

From the available makeshift armored scout cars there arose a "tank echelon" in the regiment, which simplified training and maintenance. After the war broke out these vehicles were replaced by light armored scout cars (Sd.Kfz.253). These 5.73-ton halftrack vehicles were originally developed only for the assault artillery. For their use in the divisional artillery they were given different radio equipment (Fu 8, Fu 4, Radio Speaker f, and Canister Radio b 1). Another

To march, the barrel of the 15 cm Heavy Howitzer 18 (weighing 1774 kg) had to be drawn back onto the mount.

Before the war broke out, some motorized artillery units in the armored divisions received Panzerkampfwagen I tanks (MG) (Sd.Kfz.102) as transitional equipment for the not yet available armored scout cars. The performance, armor, and equipment of these vehicles corresponded only in part with the demands made by such use.

A few Panzerkampfwagen II (2 cm) (Sd.Kfz. 121) also appeared as armored scout cars in the motorized artillery of the armored divisions. They also remained with the troops for only a short time as makeshift solutions, but helped the advanced observers to gain experience.

The small Armored Command Car I (Sd.Kfz, 265) was also used as an armored scout car.

vehicle used this way was the medium armored scout car (Sd.Kfz.254), of which the troops received 128 between June 1940 and March 1941—the German Army's only armored vehicle with wheeled or tracked running gear. It was developed by the Austrian firm of Saurer in 1937. Naturally, these vehicles differed externally from the tanks. They soon became victims of enemy defenses, as their armor offered protection only from infantry-weapon fire and shell fragments. For the future the motorized artillery requested new designs for armored scout cars.

128 of the medium armored scout car (Sd.Kfz. 254) made by the Austrian Saurer Works AG were delivered to the Army as of March 1941. The vehicle weighed 6.8 tons and had armor 3 to 14.5 mm thick.

The massive halftrack towing tractors pulling the heavy guns. Here we see an 8-ton Medium Tractor KM m 11 (Sd.Kfz.7) with a 15 cm Heavy Howitzer 18 (mot.) in a parade—typical of the German Wehrmacht.

III. 1939-1940
THE FIRST WAR EXPERIENCES

Essentially, the unit structure of the division artillery of 1938 was retained. For the motorized artillery regiments of the five armored divisions as of August 1939 that comprised the regimental staff with intelligence platoon, weather troop, printing troop, music corps, and the two light units with the unit staffs, intelligence platoons, and artillery measuring troops, as well as three motorized batteries, each with four 10.5 cm Light Howitzer 18 and two machine guns. The artillery regiments of the motorized infantry divisions had three light units. There was also a heavy unit with staff, intelligence platoon, and three motorized batteries, each with four 15 cm Heavy Howitzer 18, and the motorized observation unit with staff, measuring, sound-measuring, and light-measuring battery.

In the "History of Artillery Regiment 103 / Armored Artillery Regiment 103" it is reported that, in view of the threatening danger of war at the beginning of August 1939, a "silent mobilization" was carried out, with related marching and combat drills in the war-strength unit. Reserve officers and inexperienced men helped, after eight short weeks of training, to fill existing gaps in personnel. Civilian vehicles arrived at the barracks and were prepared for wartime use. They were utilized mainly in the ammunition and maintenance units.

During the combat in Poland in September 1939 the motorized artillery gave the motorized artillery of their own attacking tanks and riflemen the necessary support. In some cases the batteries had to fight off the short-range attacks of Polish infantry and cavalry. If the combat situation was unclear they had to form hedgehogs and set up the guns so that they pointed in all four directions. The greatest difficulties, caused by the bad weather, were those of ammunition supply. Offroad-capable special vehicles for this purpose were lacking.
The campaign's experiences were evaluated thoroughly. To improve fire control, the transmission of information via telephone and radio was reorganized. A new focal point appeared in the training guidelines—fighting against tanks.

France—the enemy in the next campaign—had numerous tanks. Their appearance had to be expected anywhere. A considerable strengthening of firepower was linked with the subordination or inclusion of heavy artillery units in the artillery regiments of the armored divisions. Thus, at the end of January 1940 the II. Unit of Artillery Regiment 93 was sent to Artillery Regiment (mot.) 103 of the 4th Armored Division. On June 29, 1940, it was firmly subordinated as the III. Unit. The newly established 7th Armored Division received a motorized heavy artillery unit with two batteries of 15 cm Heavy Howitzer 18 and one battery of 10 cm cannons early in June 1940. With the 10 cm Heavy Cannon 18 shot ranges of over 19,000 could be attained. They allowed tank attacks to be covered for long periods by fire from parts of the division's artillery, as long as the attacks held ground in the depths of the enemy defenses.

In the heavy motorized artillery units, where 8-ton medium towing tractors (Sd.Kfz.7) were not available in sufficient numbers to tow the 15 cm Heavy Howitzer 18 or the 10 cm Heavy Cannon 18, 3-ton medium offroad-capable (6x4) trucks were used as a makeshift solution. The picture shows such a truck, a Henschel Type 33G 1.

During the western campaign in 1940, HL kl 6 p medium armored troop transporters (Sd.Kfz.251) were used as "light armored tractors," at least in the motorized light artillery units and by training troops of the Artillery School. This picture was taken that May during the advance of German troops into Arnheim, Netherlands.

In the telephone troops of the intelligence platoons of motorized staff batteries, the Wanderer W 14 medium offroad-capable personnel car (4x2), among others, was used as a small (light) telephone or radio car (Kfz.2).

The 2.5-ton light offroad uniform truck (6x6), or "Uniform Diesel," was used as a telephone or radio service truck (Kfz. 61), a truck for sound and light evaluation (Kfz.62), a measuring or alerting truck (Kfz.63), or an observation vehicle (Kfz.76) in the motorized artillery.

For the ammunition troops of the motorized light howitzer batteries, at war-strength eight medium offroad-capable trucks were planned for ammunition transport. If these trucks were not available then stock trucks were used.

An openly arrived battery of 10.5 cm Light Howitzer 18 (mot.) is seen during combat. In general, firing was done according to a plan, which limited the artillery's action in both space and time. The troop leader's combat tasks were the basis of this. The fast and mobile combat of armored units strongly limited the ability of motorized artillery to direct the combat according to firing plans.

That was important, particularly when the batteries equipped with howitzers changed position. The problems were the heavy weight (6434 kg) of the guns and the light weight (15.14 kg) of the shells. In all, the inclusion of heavy units in the motorized artillery regiments of the armored divisions resulted in a considerable increase in shot weights per minute of fire from 2275.2 kg to 4030.56 kg. Since the number of tanks in the divisions had simultaneously been lowered, the ratio of armored shock power and artillery firepower improved in favor of the artillery.

The fighting in France in May and June 1940 showed again that the motorized artillery, because of the nature of mobile combat for the armored divisions, often became involved in the close combat of the enemy infantry and tanks. During the fighting in the latter half of May, and particularly in the heavy fighting around the French Weygand Line, the disadvantages of the unarmored guns had already become clear. Thus, despite the strong concentration of fire, it was not possible to drive the enemy out of his heavily fortified support points and establish contact with the advancing tanks. The occupied villages had to be conquered to be able to bring up the motorized batteries. That succeeded only under great pressure, so that artillery support decreased at longer ranges. Only when fuel and ammunition were moved forward did tank attacks pick up momentum. The consumption of ammunition shows the intensity of the combat.

Artillery Regiment (mot.) 103 alone used almost 80 tons of ammunition on one day (June 5, 1940). The General of the Armored Troops, Heinz Guderian, stated in August 1940 while evaluating the experiences of the French campaign:

"The self-propelled gun mount for the light artillery units (of the armored divisions) is an undeniable necessity."

Further experience concerned technical and tactical aspects of the use of divisional artillery against the expected high numbers of French and British tank forces. The unarmored motorized artillery had been hit harder by low-flying enemy aircraft than other parts of the armored divisions during the campaign.

The Flak protection of the battery positions had to be strengthened. This was done by adding Army anti-aircraft companies with 2 cm quad guns. [text resumes near bottom of column 1, page 43]

The structure of the artillery units was also changed. Staff, intelligence platoon, measurement troop, and supply services were united in the staff battery. Some regiments received new armored scout cars (12 of them), though of Type II. The great importance of observation artillery for the armored divisions' combat, marked by quick changes of action, had been confirmed again in France. Every armored division was assigned an armored observation battery that officially belonged to the artillery regiment and was assigned tactically to cooperate with the artillery leader of the armored division. According to the "Temporary Guidelines for Application and Use of the Armored Observation Battery" of November 12, 1940 (Artillery Memo No. 19), its tasks included locating enemy artillery, battlefield surveillance, and aiming its own batteries, plus duplicating maps and issuing weather reports. According to War Strength Report No. 545 (makeshift) of September 24, 1940, an armored observation battery was composed of the battery troop, light-measuring staff, sound-measuring staff, evaluation staff, weather troop, printing troop, combat, provision, and baggage supply troops, and maintenance troop. The armored observation batteries proved themselves remarkably well in the armored divisions, but were removed from them when the armored divisions were restructured in 1943.

A 10.5 cm Light Howitzer 18 (mot.) of the IV. (light) Unit of an SS artillery regiment, which belonged to the strengthened Leibstandarte Adolf Hitler SS Division since April 1940, is seen during combat at Etienne on June 23, 1940. The motorized light artillery unit formed the basis of armored artillery in the Waffen-SS.

The weight of the 10.5 cm Light Howitzer 18 (mot.) in firing position was stated as 2015 kg. In 1938 the price of a gun of this type was 25,800 RM. Every shell (with Impact Fuze 23, aluminum version) cost about 25 RM, while the shell basket (= 10.35 RM) and transport case of fuzes (= 13.50 RM) must be added on. With the 14.81 kg howitzer shell using the 5th charge, ranges up to 9150 meters could be attained.

The 10.5 cm Light Howitzer 18 (mot.) just after being unhitched. The mount is a barrel-recoil spread type with barrel brake, fluid equalizer, mantle, pneumatic recuperator, and target indication. The two spars have firm iron spurs and one folding earth spur each.

This picture was taken during the 1940 French campaign. The 10.5 cm Light Howitzer 18 (mot.) was towed by a 5-ton medium towing tractor (Sd.Kfz.6). The gun's folding spurs can be seen clearly.

According to war strentgh records, four guns belonged to a light howitzer battery (mot.) At the maximum rate of fire (8 rounds per minute), 473.9 kg of shot mass could be fired in a minute.

[page 46, captions]
A training battery of the Artillery School was equipped with four Czech 10 cm light howitzers. The guns were designated 10 cm Light Howitzer 30 (t). They were towed by lightly armored tractors.

The 10 cm Light Howitzer 30 (t) weighed 1766 kg in firing position (3077 kg marching) and could fire an explosive shell (16 kg) to a range of 10,600 meters. The German Wehrmacht took over 158 guns of this type.

A temporary equipment description of the 10 cm Light Howitzer 30 (t), horse- or vehicle-drawn, came out on July 11, 1941, and was numbered D 370. It was described therein as a barrel-recoil gun with spring recuperator, spring equalizer, shield, and independent target indication by panoramic scope.

One job of the advanced observer in motorized artillery units and batteries was to observe his own guns' fire from far forward and keep contact with the units that cooperated with tanks. For this he often had only a medium offroad car (Kfz.17) available. Since it was not armored it had to be left under cover, which affected his cooperation with the leaders of the tanks and motorized guns.

In the pause that followed the French campaign, prescribed work was reworked and completed. Important statements on the use of motorized artillery in armored bands can be found in the "Guidelines for Command and Use of Armored Divisions" of December 3, 1940. It is stated there:

"The artillery, corresponding to the mobility of the armored divisions, must be led in a very mobile and nimble way, it must be able to give steady and effective support to the quick movements of the tank attacks."

It was required that the motorized batteries be included far forward in the marching columns, so as to let them enter the battle effectively at the right time. It was the advanced observers' (VB) task to accompany the first wave of tanks in their armored scout cars and direct "the fire of their batteries on the targets limiting the tank

From March 1940 to June 1941, 285 of the light armored scout car (Sd.Kfz. 253) were delivered. Some of them replaced the Kfz. 17 used by observers in motorized artillery units and batteries of armored divisions.

This picture was taken in the 11th Armored Division in Serbia in the spring of 1941. It shows a Medium Armored Observation Vehicle (Sd.Kfz. 245) of the I. (light) Unit of Motorized Artillery Regiment 119. The vehicle belonged to the 3rd Battery. Its radio equipment consisted of one Fu 8, one Fu 4, and one Radio Speaker Device f.

attack." The Instructions for Artillery No. 24, "Temporary Guidelines for the Training of Tank Observers and Firing from Armored Scout Cars," and No. 25, "Temporary Guidelines for the Action and Use of the Artillery in the Armored Division," issued early in 1941, also expressed concepts of specifically mobile combat command. Artillery leaders were required to think ahead as they acted. Strict rules for artillery use were not given. Essentially, the strongest possible parts of the division's artillery were to work closely for the direct support of the tanks. It was stated literally:

"The...units accompany the tank attack with observed fire, break emerging enemy resistance, and fight down enemy antitank weapons."

It was stressed that the variety of tasks must not lead to a division of artillery fire. The lack of armored self-propelled gun mounts was recognized as a definite disadvantage. Because of the unarmored tractors, changing positions to the fore could only succeed when the guns had won and cleaned out the land. The use of the armored scout cars also took up a lot of space. To be sure, not all units had these vehicles.

The experience gained in the 1930-40 campaigns helped to emphasize qualitative values of the artillery in the armored divisions more strongly. On the other hand, the experiences in the Balkans in the spring of 1941 brought nothing new, aside from the details of use in the mountains.

The 1.5-ton Mercedes-Benz G 3a light offroad-capable (6x4) truck (above) and Büssing-NAG 31 were used in the artillery units (mot.) and observation units (mot.) as telephone or radio service trucks (Kfz. 61), large telephone, radio, or print-shop trucks, sound reception, sound- and light-measuring trucks (Kfz. 62), measuring or alerting trucks (Kfz. 63), calculating trucks (Kfz. 64), and observation trucks (Kfz. 76).

The medium offroad-capable (4x4) personnel cars of various types were used with closed bodies (Kfz. 17) as substitutes for lacking armored scout cars. They were distributed to unit staffs and batteries.

An 8-ton KM m 11 medium towing tractor (Sd.Kfz.7) tows trucks of an ammunition squad over a rough stretch of road—a typical picture from the eastern front. Weather, road, and terrain conditions influenced the mobility of the motorized artillery there more than in other theaters of war. Supply of ammunition and fuel was hit especially hard.

IV. 1941-1942
PERFORMANCE LIMITS OF MOTORIZED FIELD ARTILLERY

The preparations for the campaign against Soviet Russia up to the summer of 1941 resulted in a considerable increase in the number of armored divisions. In June 1941 there were 17 armored divisions in all on the eastern front, divided—along with the motorized infantry divisions—into four armored groups. The motorized artillery had been built up comparably. For them, in addition to their basic combat tasks as described in the previous chapter, there arose a new essential task in antitank defense. It is significant that the efficiency of the Russian armored troops in 1941 was comparatively meager. Yet they possessed a very large number of tanks, including the hitherto unknown T-34 and KW types. Their appearance had to be reckoned with at all times and places, which led to local crises and defeats. Technologically, the Army's antitank troops were no longer able to provide effective antitank action, which necessarily required greater involvement of the divisional artillery. Now the disadvantages of their being equipped almost exclusively with howitzers became apparent. The range of the standard gun (10.5 cm Light Howitzer 18) in direct fire was only about 500 meters. Armored targets at greater ranges had to be straddled. The howitzers' slower rate of fire (6-8 rounds per minute) and the great elevation of fire, as well as the strong

A 15 cm Heavy Howitzer 18 (mot.) is seen just after firing. During the war it was seen that the gun was not mobile enough; its range was less than that of the Russian cannon-howitzers (max. 17,260 m). Besides, every gun was to be suited to antitank use, which could be done only within limits.

Among the tasks of the motorized artillery during tank attacks was the blinding of the enemy's antitank defenses and artillery observation posts. For the Heavy Howitzer 18, the 15 cm Shell 19 Fog with 23 Fog Impact Fuze was available. It weighed 39 kg, and its range was stated as 13,500 meters. When it hit, a cloud of fog with a diamater of 40 meters was created, remained effective up to 40 seconds, and then blew away.

The 10 cm Heavy Cannon 18 (mot.) was the "long arm" of the motorized artillery regiments of the armored divisions. Its great range of 19,075 meters with the 10 cm Shell 19 and 10 cm Shell 19 FES allowed it to support its own armored units for long distances when following withdrawing enemy forces.

The advanced observers of the motorized artillery were to accompany the advancing attacks of the tanks and motorized riflemen under all conditions. Their place was in the tank units with their lightly armored scout cars (Sd.Kfz. 253). Their radio equipment, like that of the motorized artillery, had been changed (Fu 8, Fu 4, and Radio Device f). The insufficient range of the UKW radios in vocal contact was criticized repeatedly.

production of fire and smoke on firing diminished their chances of success in combat against tanks, and the considerable weight in firing position made turning the gun hard for the crew in order to take tanks appearing from the side or the rear under fire. There was suitable ammunition for antitank use. It included the 10 cm antitank shell, which when fired with the 5th or 6th charge, was able to penetrate 52 to 59 mm of armor plate at a range of 500 meters. Just before the campaign began, hollow-charge ammunition was issued to the troops. With its help, regardless of the range, 90 mm of armor could be penetrated. For the 15 cm Heavy Howitzer 18, a 27.5 kg 15 cm Shell 39 HL/A was available, with a penetrating power of 160 mm of armor plate. Here, too, the range in direct fire was below 500 meters. Only the 10 cm Heavy Cannon 18, one battery of which was in each heavy unit of the motorized artillery regiments, could fight off tanks at longer ranges. The 10 cm red antitank shell, with a respectable muzzle velocity of 682 to 822 meters per second, could penetrate 100 to 138 mm of armor at a range of 1000 meters. At about 5.5 tons, though, the cannon was twice as heavy as a 10.5 cm Light Howitzer 18, a decided disadvantage in antitank defense. The attacking tanks went around the guns or rolled over them, and the number of losses added up. The Chief of the Organizational Unit in the Army High Command, Generalleutnant Walter Buhl, had to accept a 50% reduction of the combat strength of the armored divisions as early as August 1941. The loss of towing tractors was considerable, which was no surprise, what with the road and weather conditions in the eastern theater of war. Despite the vigorous repair service, by mid-September 1941 a 30% shortage of tractors had to be reckoned with. The fuel situation created further problems,

In the foreground is a medium T-34 tank (1939 model) of the Red Army, and in back a 3-ton HL kl 6 light tractor (Sd.Kfz.11) of the motorized artillery. On the eastern front their guns were more strongly linked to the antitank forces than in other theaters of war. The almost complete equipping with howitzers, though, limited their effectiveness to ranges under 500 meters.

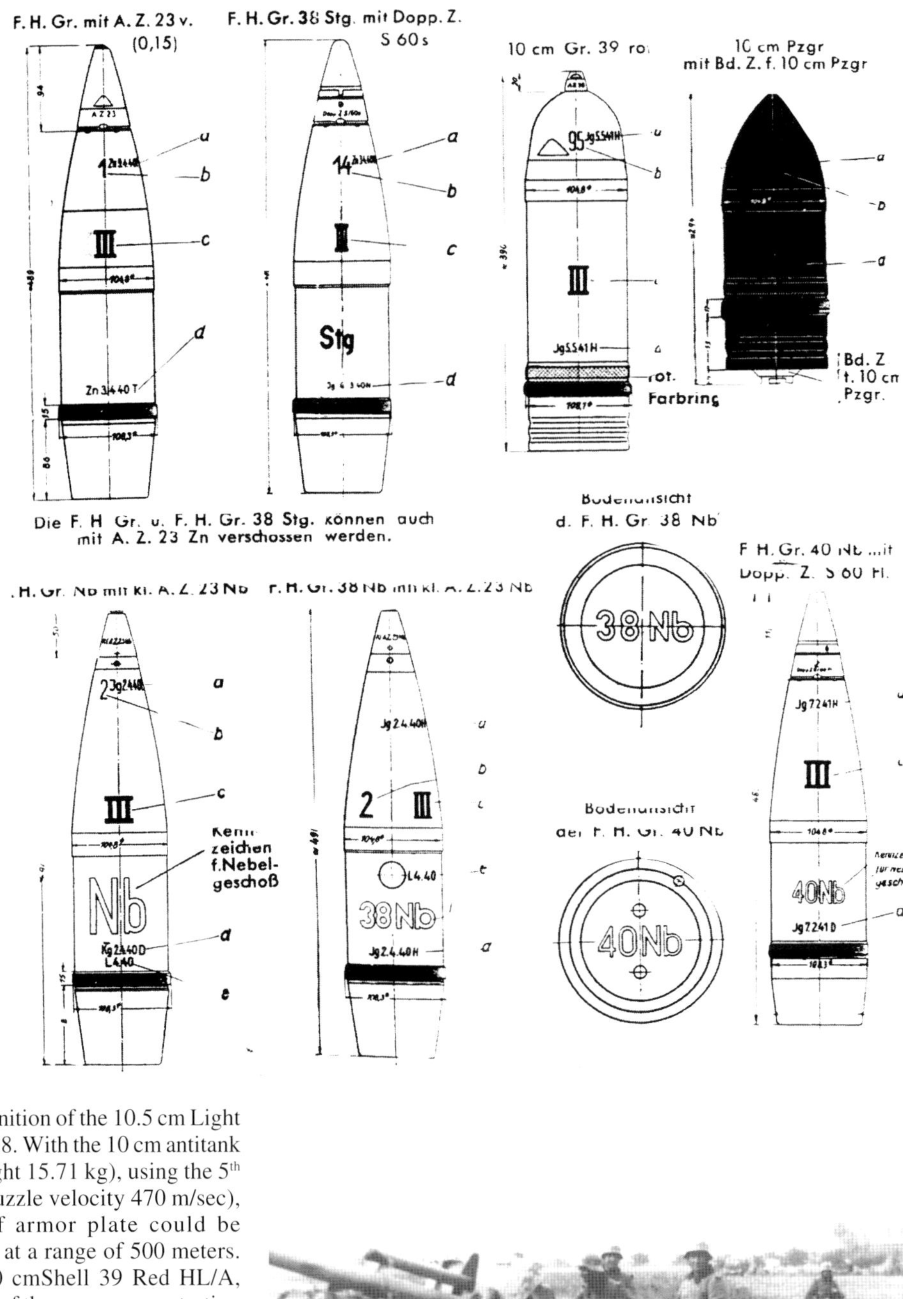

The ammunition of the 10.5 cm Light Howitzer 18. With the 10 cm antitank shell (weight 15.71 kg), using the 5th charge (muzzle velocity 470 m/sec), 52 mm of armor plate could be penetrated at a range of 500 meters. For the 10 cmShell 39 Red HL/A, regardless of the range, a penetrating power of 80 mm of armor was attained.

The crew of a 15 cm Heavy Howitzer 18 (mot.) moves the right spar into position.

The ammunition of the 15 cm Heavy Howitzer 18. To fire on concrete and armored targets, the 15 cm Shell 19 Concrete (weighing 43.5 kg) was available. With it, concrete thicknesses to 450 mm could be broken. Later the 15 cm Shell 39 HL was added for antitank use. It was capable of penetrating up to 130 mm of armor plate.

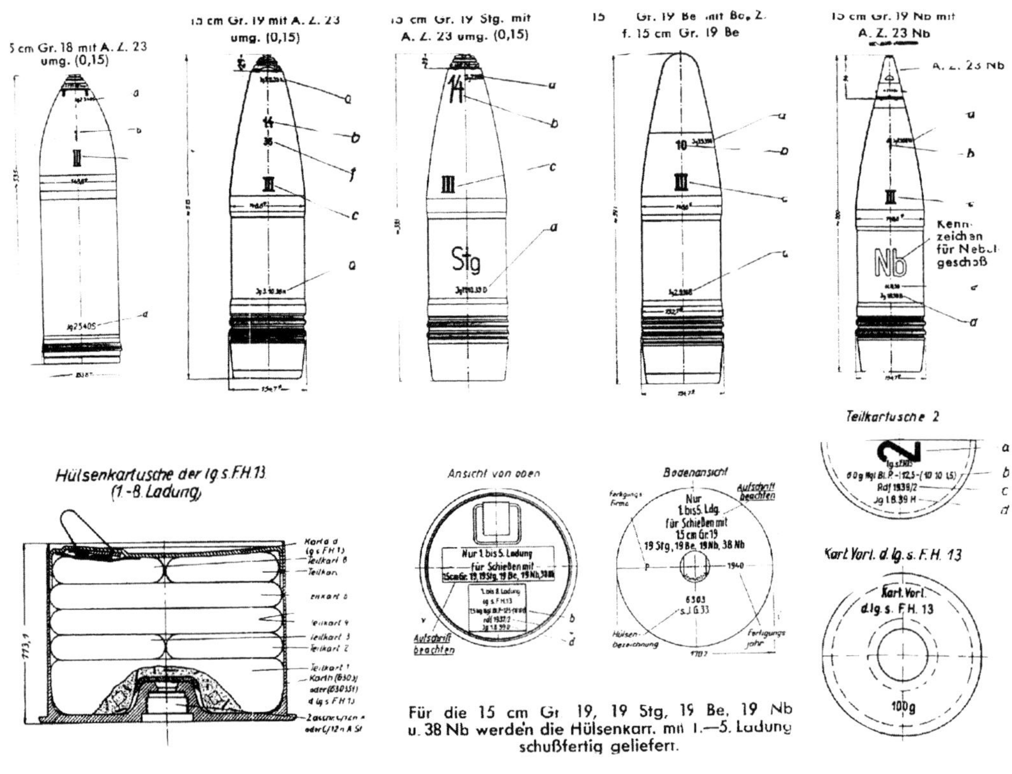

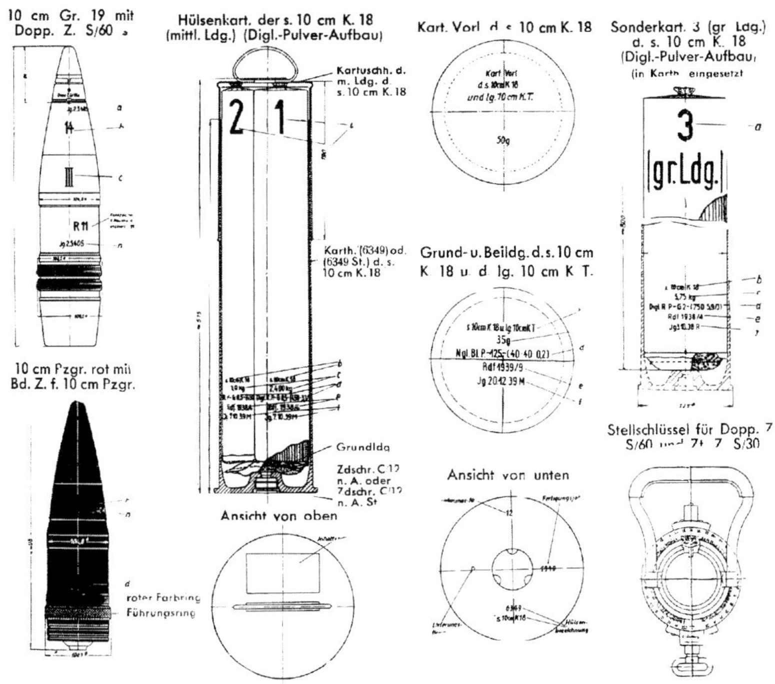

The ammunition of the 10 cm Heavy Cannon 18. With the 10 cm Red Antitank Shell, using a medium charge, 112 mm of armor could be penetrated at 500 meters. When the heavy charge was used, a depth of 155 mm was achieved. The weight of the 10 cm Red Antitank Shell was stated as 15.6 kg, the muzzle velocity as 602 or 822 m/sec.

Guns of a 10 cm heavy cannon battery in firing position.

Staff Battery (mot.) of an Artillery unit (mot.) of an Armored Division, according to War Strength Report No. 585 of February 1, 1941

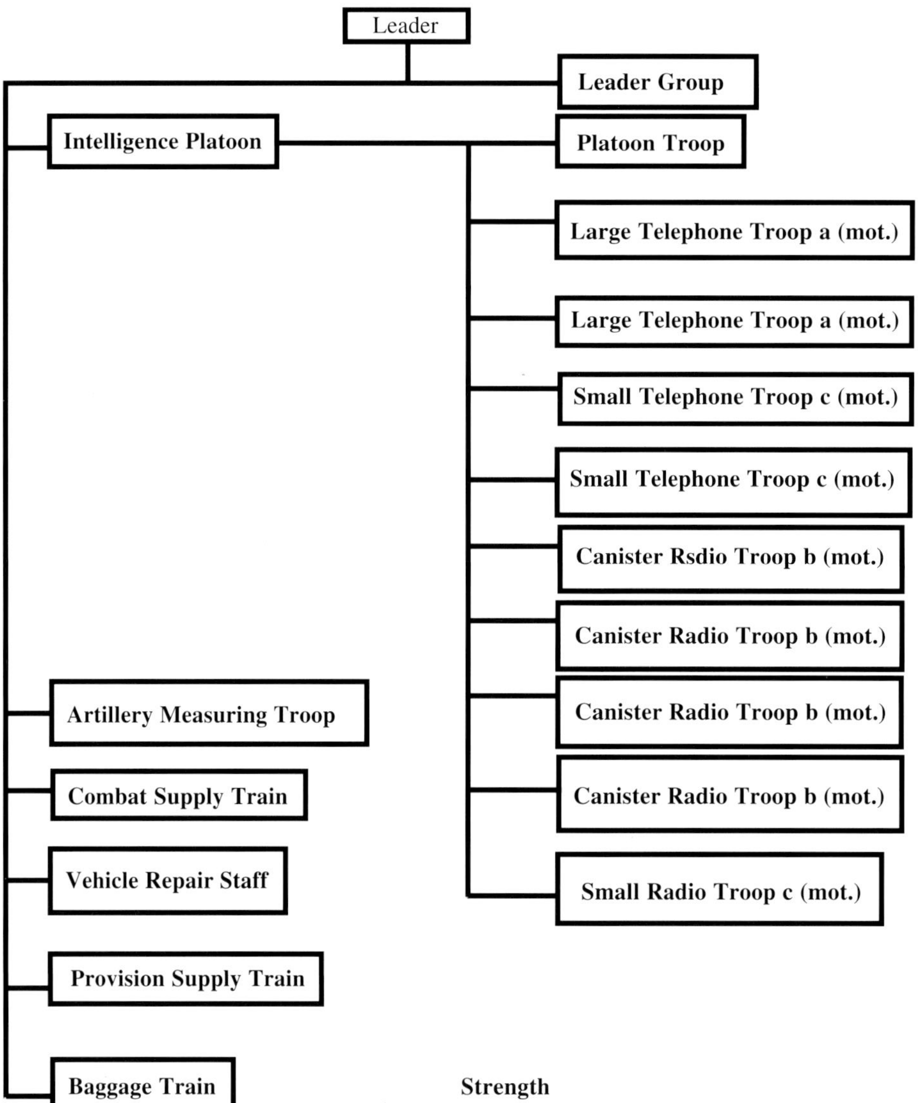

Strength
2/2/20/91
10 motorcycles, two with sidecars
30 personnel cars and trucks
1 medium armored scout car (Sd.Kfz.254)

Artillery observers of the motorized artillery carry their portable radios, maps, and other equipment. In every motorized or armored observation vehicle, a portable Canister Radio (frequency range 2.5-3.5 Mhz) was carried.

The†"Uniform Diesel," as a 2.5-ton offroad-capable (6x6) truck, was among the best German vehicles of this type. In the motorized artillery units of the armored divisions, this truck was found in various versions.

Battery of Heavy Howitzers
(up to four guns) (mot.Z.)
of an armored division, according to War Strength Directive No. 463 of February 1, 1941.

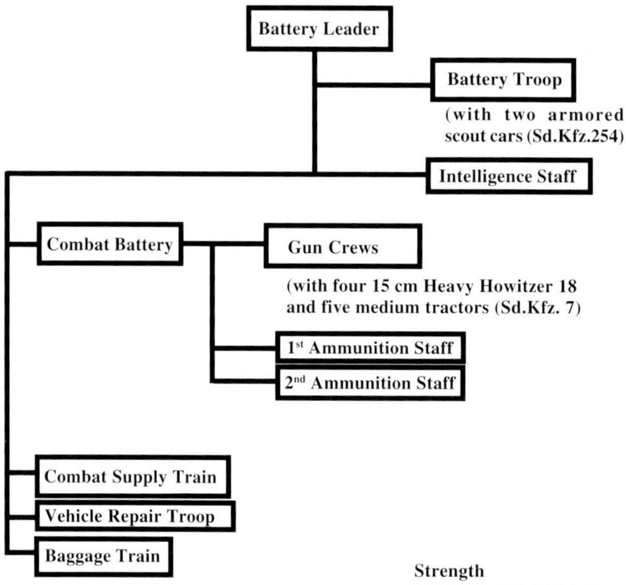

Strength
(weapons and vehicles)
5/25/138
2 heavy machine guns
4 15 cm Heavy Howitzer 18
2 armored scout cars
5 medium trailers (Sd.Kfz.7)
27 passenger cars and trucks
11 motorcycles, two with sidecars

A 15 cm Heavy Howitzer 18 (mot.) is being serviced. Typical of this gun were the pierced steel wheels (1230 x 140 mm). On a smooth roadbed with a dry surface, they allowed marching speeds up to 40 kph.

Battery of 10 cm Cannons (up to 4 guns) (mot.Z.)
of an Armored Division, according to War Strength Bulletin No. 457 of February 1, 1941

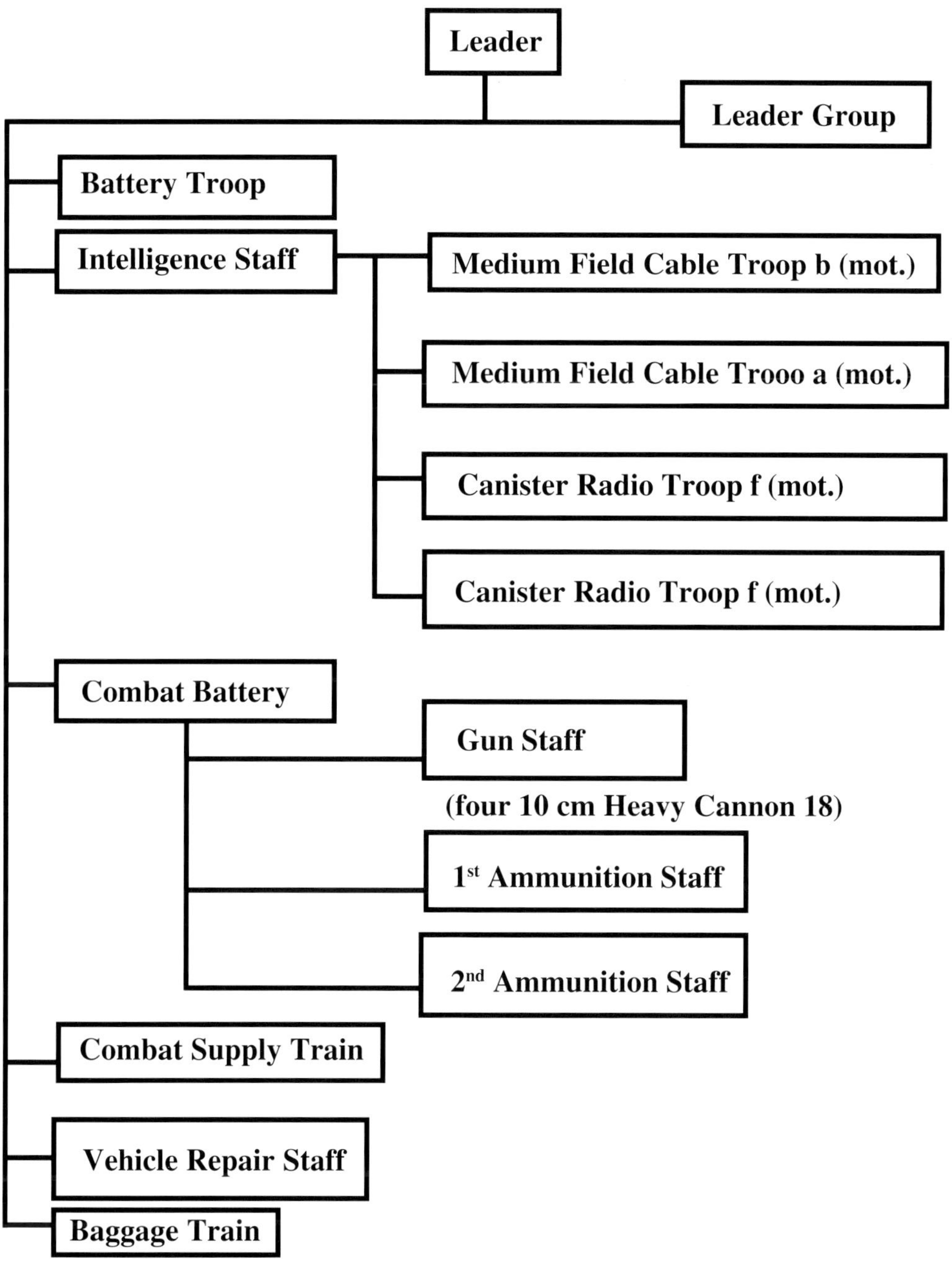

The 10 cm Heavy Cannon 18 (mot.) weighed 5642 kg in firing position. It was present in the armored divisions to the end of World War II as one battery with four guns. The unfavorable gun weight and shot weight (10 cm Shell 19, only 15.14 kg) was often criticized. The range was also too low, which is why a 12.8 cm cannon with a range of 23,000 meters was prepared toward the war's end.

especially in Army Group Center, where numerous motorized units were concentrated at the end of September; the fuel-supply situation became complicated. The armored divisions' combat readiness suffered from this, partiaularly that of the motorized artillery.

The Red Army's counteroffensive, which began on December 5, 1941, put the German troops before Moscow on the defensive. The bitter winter made their situation worse. The 4th Armored Division and its subordinated bands alone lost 15 guns and launchers, 19 tractors, and about 240 trucks on December 6 and 7, 1941. The question of whether the high losses during the withdrawal were avoidable was answered in the division's history as follows:

"At first it is sure that in every kind of withdrawal a considerable number of the completely outworn vehicles, and the guns with them, must be lost. It was impossible to tow back or repair the many damaged vehicles."

The war structure report of the 4th Armored Division on December 13, 1941, shows Artillery Regiment 103 with the staff battery, Armored Observation Battery 324, the 5th Company, Army Anti-Aircraft Battalion 66, the II. Unit of Artillery Regiment (mot.) 103 with ten 10.5 cm Light Howitzer 18 guns, and the III. Unit of Artillery Regiment (mot.) 103 with eight 15 cm Heavy Howitzer 18.

A photo from the winter war of 1941 in the east. The heavy howitzer, weighing over six tons in marching trim, broke through the frozen road surface because of its heavier specific ground pressure compared to that of the tractor. In critical combat situations, particularly during withdrawal fighting, this could mean that the gun had to be left behind.

The tractors of the motorized artillery often were used to tow trucks that got stuck. In the winter of 1941-42 it took a lot of trouble to guarantee the troops' mobility.

An 8-ton KM m 11 Medium Tractor (Sd.Kfz.7) is seen during a thaw. The constant overstraining of the complicated vehicles led to numerous breakdowns. In all, 2469 tractors of all types broke down in 1941.

The Red Army captured this 8-ton KM m 11 Medium Tractor (Sd.Kfz.7) in the area around Tula in the latter half of November 1941.

To assure the troops' mobility in the storm conditions, native sleds and panje wagons had to be taken over. In addition, similar vehicles were built in the troops' workshops. Special sleds were used to transport the guns.

The I. Unit was missing. It was disbanded for lack of guns and tractors.

The motorized artillery regiments of the armored divisions showed a colorful picture at the beginning of 1942 regarding their weapons, vehicles, and equipment. Under the extreme winter conditions in the east, it had been necessary to use horses and sleds to be able to attain at least a certain degree of mobility. A great portion of their specified numbers of tractors, trucks, and special trailers, as well as guns, were wrecks lining the withdrawal routes, had been captured by the Red Army, or were in the workshops for lack of spare parts. At this time it would have been hard to tell the artillery units of armored and infantry divisions apart. This applied not only to their appearance, but also to their use. The meager supply of new guns, vehicles, and equipment made the reorganization of the motorized artillery harder. Only 45 of the 10.5 cm Light Howitzer 18 guns were delivered in January 1942, and only 104 in the following month. The situation was similar for the 15 cm Heavy Howitzer 18 and the 10 cm Heavy Cannon 18, of which the monthly average of deliveries in 1941-42 was 81 and 16, respectively. This was not enough to replace the losses of the previous year. The number of German guns decreased, and many urgently needed repair due to overuse of their barrels. Thus, for a long time complete batteries received captured Russian cannons and howitzers. The following types were often found:

- 76.2 mm Division Cannon 36 (F-22), designated 7.62 cm Cannon 296(r)-russ. 36-
- 122 mm Division Howitzer 10/30, designated 12.2 cm Light Howitzer 388(r)-russ. 10/30-

To replace the 10.5 cm Light Howitzer 18, of 17,260 to 13,580 meters could be fired on. The explosive shell, though, weighed only 6.23 kg.

The performance of the 7.62 cm Cannon 297(r)-russ.39-, which was used like the 7.62 cm Cannon 296(r), was similar. The guns had been captured in large numbers during the combat in the summer of 1941.

The Russian 122 mm Division Howitzer 38 was used by some motorized artillery regiments as 12.2 cm Heavy Howitzer 396(r)-russ.38-. The gun weighed 2200 kg in firing position and, with the 21.76-kg heavy explosive shell, could fire effectively on targets up to 12,100 meters away.

- 122 mm Division Howitzer 38, designated 12.2 cm Heavy Howitzer 396(r)-russ. 38-

Later in the course of the war, ammunition began to be produced for the last-named gun, which emphasizes its importance.

The use of Russian cannons in the divisional artillery had a positive effect on their ability to take part successfully in antitank defense. On the other hand, the use of these guns for purely artilleristic tasks was debated, although they generally had greater shot ranges. In the "Artilleristische Rundschaü of September 1942 experiences with Russian cannons were evaluated. In comparison with the light howitzer, the trajectory of the shells was not variable enough. This made the choice of firing positions and firing on hidden targets harder. The effect of the 6.5-kg explosive shells was too meager, and on long shots the advanced artillery observers could not see where they hit because of the comparatively small clouds of smoke. This complicated fire control, which in turn negatively influenced targeting accuracy and thus the effectiveness of the artillery fire. Despite these failings, captured guns and ammunition had to go on being used. German-made replacements came only later. For example, the Artillery Regiment of the 4th Armored Division received its I. Unit with twelve 10.5 cm Light Howitzer 18 in July 1942. The specified number of 15 cm Heavy Howitzers and 10 cm Heavy Cannon 18 reached the troops only in October 1942. The situation was similar in the other armored and motorized units, if they were not intended for the offensive operations on the south part of the eastern front.

In place of the 15 cm Heavy Howitzer 18 (mot.), some batteries of the heavy units received the captured 15.2 cm Cannon Howitzer 433/1(r)-russ. 37-. Its only advantage was its greater shot range of 17,260 meters with the 43.5-kg heavy explosive shell.

A Russian village street in the southern sector of the eastern front, seen in the spring of 1942. The spring thaw turned roads and streets into deep mud at first, which strongly limited the mobility of the motorized artillery in the armored divisions.

V. 1942-1943
THE ARMORED ARTILLERY ORIGINATES

On March 23, 1942, the artillery in the armored divisions was renamed "Panzerartillerie," according to a directive from the General Army office. Artillery Regiment (mot.) 103 of the 4th Armored Division received a corresponding order early in May 1942. From then on it bore the designation Armored Artillery Regiment 103. At the same time, Armored Observation Battery 324 was given the number 103. The renumbering did not affect its weapons, vehicles, or equipment. Self-propelled mounts were not yet available. On January 23, Hitler had called for the development of guns on self-propelled mounts, but there was a lack of suitable chassis. At the armament conference early in April 1942 Hitler declared:

"The development of self-propelled mounts shall be hastened, protection only against splinter effects, 30% weight reserve maintained, the meaning of the self-propelled mounts can until next spring be such that their going into production until then is necessary under conditions. The development is, when possible, to be limited to available mounts, or at least available individual parts (except the Tiger)."

At first, though, captured armored vehicles had to be used. Especially suitable was the French Lorraine 38 L supply tractor. From May 23 to 25 another conference on this subject took place. The minister for armaments and war production, Albert Speer, noted:

"The presentation by Colonels Feuchtinger, Schneider, and Esser, along with Colonel Hartmann, about self-propelled mounts on tractors means that all the still available 160 Lorraine tractors are to be rebuilt into self-propelled mounts, specifically: 60 light howitzers, 40 Heavy Howitzer 13, and 60 antitank guns.

The Führer needs some of these self-propelled mounts extremely urgently, particularly those for the Heavy Howitzer 13, for a special action by Rommel."

In July and August 1942 30 of these vehicles, designated 15 cm Heavy Howitzer 13/1 (Sfl.) on Gun Car Lorraine Tractor (f) (Sd.Kfz.135/1), were hastily shipped to North Africa. Due to enemy attacks only 23 arrived there. The priority of the armored units of the Army in the North African theater of war for equipping with armored self-propelled mounts had various reasons.
Because of the terrain conditions, the close link of tanks and artillery in the mobile warfare preferred there was very important. There was little cover. The non-armored tractors and guns of the two armored artillery regiments—16 (15th Armored Division) and 155 (21st Armored Division)—suffered particularly from enemy fire. For example, during the defense against the British attack operation "Crusader" in November 1941, the

Artillery Regiment (mot.) 190 of the 90th Light African Division of the German Afrika Korps was equipped mainly with captured guns of British and Russian origin. There were also guns left behind by the Italians, like these 7.5 cm Cannon 248 (i)-ital. 75/32 Mod.37-. They could attain a range of 12,580 meters.

A 15 cm Heavy Howitzer 18 (mot.) of the III. (heavy) Unit, Artillery Regiment (mot.) 33, is seen during the attack at Tobruk in June 1942. The regiment belonged to the 15th Armored Division of the German Afrika Korps.

According to War Strength Report No. 463, the heavy howitzer battery (of four guns, mot.Z) of an armored division had two radio trucks (Kfz.17/1) in each battery troop. This picture was taken in North Africa in 1941. One Kfz.17/1 has broken down and must be towed to a workshop.

German Afrika Korps' units lost 41 guns (40% of all they had) and ten heavy tractors in just two weeks. With the help of the self-propelled mounts, though only provisional, the efficiency of the armored artillery would improve. In a report on the combat strength and weapon supplies of the 21st Armored Division for the time from May to September 1942, the setting up of a heavy howitzer battery with 15 cm Heavy Howitzer 13 guns in Artillery Regiment 155 was mentioned.

The 64 15 cm Heavy Howitzer 13 guns still in the defensive zones were also prepared for installation on Lorraine tractors. The old guns from World War I surely no longer fulfilled the wishes of the armored artillery. Still, it could fire the 42-kg Heavy Shell 12 (VII. Charge) to a distance of 8675 meters. By the Army Weapons Office, Paris Branch (Construction Command Becker), 72 more self-propelled artillery mounts were produced and assigned to the strengthened Brigade West. The brigade was used on June 15, 1943, near Rennes, France, to reconstitute the 21st Armored Division, which had been wiped out in Africa. Armored Artillery Regiment 931, equipped with Lorraine gun tractors (f) (Sd.Kfz.135/1), was renamed Armored Artillery Regiment 155.
In connection with the rebuilding of self-propelled artillery mounts, the Becker

In loose formation, the light tractors with light howitzers of the I. (light) Unit, Artillery Regiment (mot.) 33 of the 15th Armored Division follow the tanks. In the open, coverless terrain, the unarmored vehicles and guns and their crews were especially exposed to the enemy's gunfire. This picture was taken in North Africa at the end of March 1942.

The same was true of the guns of the III. (heavy) units of the artillery regiments (mot.). Lightly armored self-propelled artillery mounts were planned for use by the German Afrika Korps. This picture shows an 8-ton KM m 11 Medium Tractor with 15 cm Heavy Howitzer 18 (mot.). On November 18, 1941, the Korps had reported having 20 guns of this type.

Construction Command built 30 large radio and observation tanks on Lorraine tractors (f). Of the 60 10.5 cm Light Howitzer 18 (sfl.) on Lorraine Tractor gun cars (f) planned in the spring of 1942, only twelve were completed. Another temporary vehicle for the armored artillery was the 10.5 cm Light Howitzer 18/3 on B-2 Gun Car (f) that was delivered by the firm Rheinmetall-Borsig GmbH. Sixteen of them were built. Others of these rebuildings were the 10.5 cm Light Howitzer 18 (sfl.) on Gun Car 39 H (f) (48 built) and the 10.5 cm Light Howitzer 16 (sfl.) on Gun Car FCM (f) (12 built). Lesser known were the self-propelled artillery mounts on captured British armored chassis, which were fitted with the 10.5 cm Light Howitzer 16 and 15 cm Heavy Howitzer 13. There were also armored observation and ammunition vehicles used in 1941 by the V. unit of the Artillery Regiment of the 227th Infantry Division. In October 1941, as the III. Unit, Artillery Regiment (mot.) 140, it joined the 22nd Armored Division, which was being formed.

In 1942, armored artillery regiments that included batteries or units with self-propelled mounts were the exception. The variety of makeshift solutions that used captured armored vehicles is remarkable. The need for armored gun cars in the artillery of the armored divisions, as has been seen in other units, was not basically new. Until this point, their realization failed for lack of sufficient production capacity in the tank-building industry. But in 1942 an essentially different situation arose. Great numbers of captured tanks were available, and a new generation of tanks appeared in the armored units. The most important German tanks, these being the Type II, 38(t), III, and IV, were confronted in battle against the modern

A 15 cm Heavy Howitzer 13/1 (Sfl.) on Lorraine Tractor Gun Car (f) (Sd.Kfz.135/1) is displayed. The chassis was that of the armored Supply Tractor 37L, some 300 of which were captured during the 1940 French campaign.

This picture clearly shows the comparatively small size of the Lorraine Tractor (f) gun car with the 15 cm Heavy Howitzer 13/1 (Sfl.). The armor was 5 to 11 mm thick. The vehicle's weight (about 8.5 tons) was correspondingly light.

15 cm armored howitzers of the Fast Brigade West are seen in France in June 1943. They belonged to an armored artillery brigade of this unit, known briefly as Armored Artillery Regiment 931 and incorporated into the reconstituted 21st Armored Division in July of that year.

A 15 cm Heavy Howitzer 13/1 (Sfl.) on a Lorraine Tractor (f) gun car (Sd.Kfz.135/1) was captured by the British in North Africa.

A good look at the 15 cm Heavy Howitzer 13/1 (Sfl.). According to plans from 1928, there were 61 of these guns on hand, still known as the long 15 cm Heavy Howitzer 13. Until they were replaced by the 15 cm Heavy Howitzer 18 they were used by the heavy units of the artillery regiments.

The armored artillery regiment of the strengthened Fast Brigade West is seen at Versailles in mid-June 1943.

Hauptmann Alfred Becker stands before a 10.5 cm Light Howitzer 18/4 (Sfl.) on a Lorraine Tractor (f) gun car. Becker had already been active in 1940 in the preparation of self-propelled artillery mounts based on captured tank chassis. In 1942 he was sent to the Altmärkische Kettenfabrik GmbH to utilize his experience in the building of such vehicles.

The 10.5 cm Light Howitzer 18/4 (Sfl.) on the Lorraine (f) gun car weighed 7.7 tons and reached a top speed of 52 kph. Twenty rounds of ammunition for the gun was carried.

For the FCM gun car (f), the 10.5 cm Light Howitzer 16 was used. The obsolete gun could still fire 7200 meters after being installed in the self-propelled mount. The armor of the 12.8-ton vehicle was 10 to 40 mm thick. It was powered by a 4-cylinder Diesel engine (83 HP) that allowed a top speed of 24 kph.

A 10.5 cm Light Howitzer 16 (Sfl.) on the chassis of the British MK VI 736 (e) light tank was a special artillery vehicle built on the initiative of Hauptmann Alfred Becker in 1940.

Hauptmann Alfred Becker with the crew of a series-production gun car with the 10.5 cm Light Howitzer 16 (Sfl.). The chassis for these gun mounts were captured British tanks. On May 29, 1941, an artillery unit was included as the 15th (Assault Gun) Battery in Artillery Regiment 227 of the 227th Infantry Division. Among others, it included twelve 10.5 cm Light Howitzer 16 guns on MK VI 736 (e) chassis. Because of its use in an infantry division this battery did not belong to the armored artillery.

In the 15th (Assault Gun) Battery of the artillery regiment there were also four armored scout cars on chassis of the MK VI light British tank in action.

Many captured vehicles were used to transport ammunition. This picture shows a French S 307 (f), or Somua MCG towing tractor used by the ammunition staff of a light self-propelled howitzer battery.

The Becker building command built 40 small armored scout cars on U.S. 630 (f) ammunition tractor chassis. Vehicles of this type were captured in large numbers during the 1940 French campaign.

Parts of a light howitzer battery are on the march. The guns were towed by 5-ton BN 9 medium towing tractors (Sd.Kfz.6). Unless otherwise ordered, the tachometer limits or aircraft marching depth were to be maintained.

This picture was taken in the southern sector of the eastern front in the summer of 1942. The motorized artillery can be seen working closely together to accompany tanks on an attack. An urgent task was knocking out enemy antitank weapons, tanks, and artillery. Success or failure depended to a great degree on the ability of the firing observer.

Vehicles and guns of a light motorized artillery unit follow the tanks deep into the enemy's territory. These are 3-ton HL kl 6 light towing tractors (Sd.Kfz.11) towing 10.5 cm light howitzers. Because of the unarmored tractors, changes of artillery positions depended on the ground gained by the infantry.

Here a 10.5 cm Light Howitzer 18 (mot.) is being loaded. Separate ammunition was used for the gun, consisting of the cartridge case with 1st to 6th charge and the howitzer shell itself. The empty (brass) case weighed 1.6 kg, the charge at most 1.06 kg; the shell's weight was listed as 14.81 kg.

A 10.5 cm Light Howitzer 18 (mot.) in firing position. Effective firing was divided into disturbing fire (single or group fire at irregular intervals), neutralizing fire (fire attacks and disturbing fire by predetermined plan), and destructive fire (fire attack with accompanying group or position fire, or destructive fire at varying intervals).

An 8-ton KM m 11 medium towing tractor (Sd.Kfz.7) towing a 15 cm Heavy Howitzer 18 (mot.) is on the move. Changing artillery positions depended chiefly on the success and progress of tank attacks. Close contact between the tank forces and the cooperating artillery units was striven for.

Army anti-aircraft units, when available in the armored divisions, were a part of the division's artillery. A few were included in motorized artillery or armored artillery regiments. Their basic division into two heavy and one light batteries was maintained. In a heavy battery there were four 8.8 cm Anti-Aircraft Gun 36 or 37 towed by the dependable 8-ton KM m 11 medium tractor (Sd.Kfz.7).

For the standard explosive shells of the 15 cm heavy howitzer two different fuzes were used: the Impact Fuze 23 with adjustable ignition delay (0.8 seconds), and the Double Fuze S/60 with a maximum time of 60 seconds. The first type, with their delay, could be used with the effect of mines. The latter could be used to fire on high targets, such as balloons, and for zeroing in amongst unfavorable terrain conditions.

The 10 cm heavy cannon is ready to march. It was towed individually on motorized marches like the 15 cm Heavy Howitzer 18 (mot.).

Russian T-34 and KW tanks, with qualitative demands that could not be met permanently by modernizing their armor and weapons or providing better training and combat experience for their crews. New tanks arose. These included the VK 3001 (the later Panzer V or†"Panther," Sd.Kfz.171) and the VK 4501 (the later Panzer VI, or†"Tiger," Sd.Kfz.181). They reached the troops at the end of 1942 or the beginning of 1943. With series production of the modernized Panzer III (Sd.Kfz.141/1) in full swing, the main goal was to compensate for the rising numbers of total losses and fill the gap until sufficient numbers of new tanks were available. Part of the Panzer III and IV production capacity would thus be available for the production of self-propelled artillery mounts in the near future. The same was true of the Panzer II tank (Sd.Kfz.121). Early in 1942 the development of self-propelled artillery mounts had begun. There were many reasons for this: The experiences of the previous campaigns had confirmed the correctness of the tactical-technical demands for such vehicles from prewar days. In view of the considerably increased firepower of all defensive weapons to which the armored divisions were particularly exposed, the development and construction of armored gun cars now was an urgent task. First, the significance of the armored artillery in fighting against antitank weapons had increased, and second, the guns of the armored artillery itself required sufficient protection. They needed:

- Offroad capability comparable to that of the tanks.
- Ability to change positions and be ready to fire in the shortest time, for example, to knock out recurring opposition quickly.
- All-round fire for artillery weapons; turning the entire vehicle did not fulfill this requirement in an artilleristic sense.

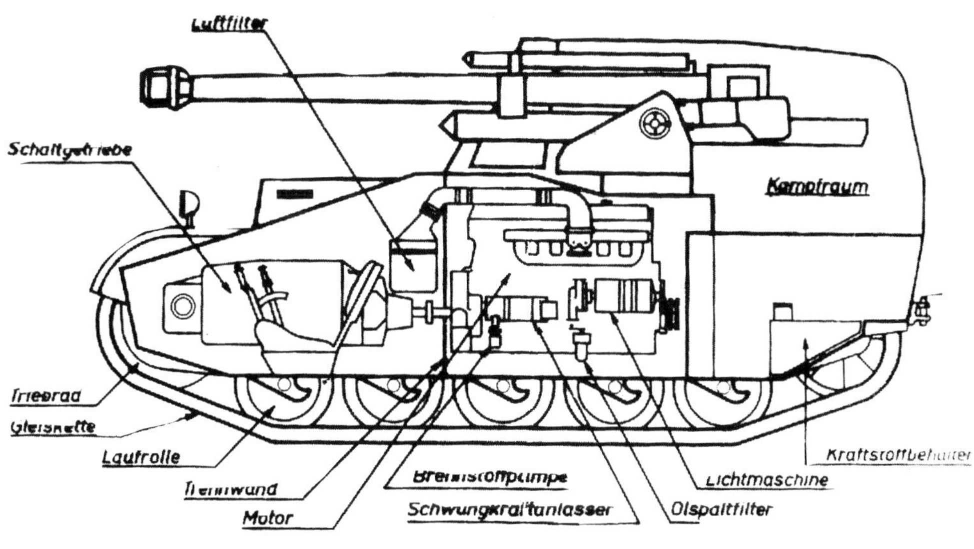

A drawing of the 10.5 cm Light Howitzer 18/II on a Type II armored self-propelled mountfrom the textbook for driver training of Instructional Staff T of Artillery School II in Jüterbog (as of December 1942).

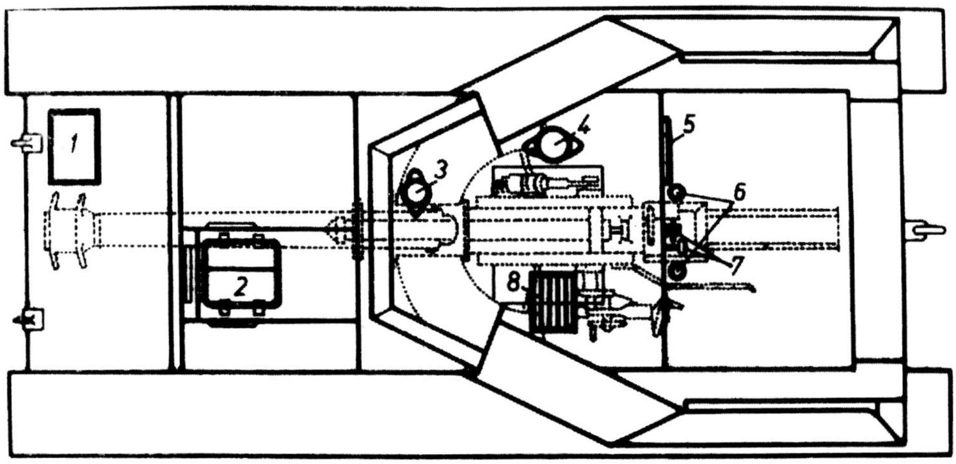

1. Steering … support brake flap
2. Driver's entry hatch
3. Coolant filler cap
4. Oil filler cap
5. Ventilator lid
6. Fuel filler caps
7. Aiming crank attachment
8. Adjustable air vent

Top view of the 10.5 cm Light Howitzer 18/II on armored Self-propelled Mount II (as of December 1942).

Displaying the wooden mockup of the 10.5 cm Light Howitzer 18/II on Self-propelled Mount II. The decision to use the chassis of the Panzer II (2 cm) (Sd.Kfz.121) for a self-propelled mount was made in July 1942.

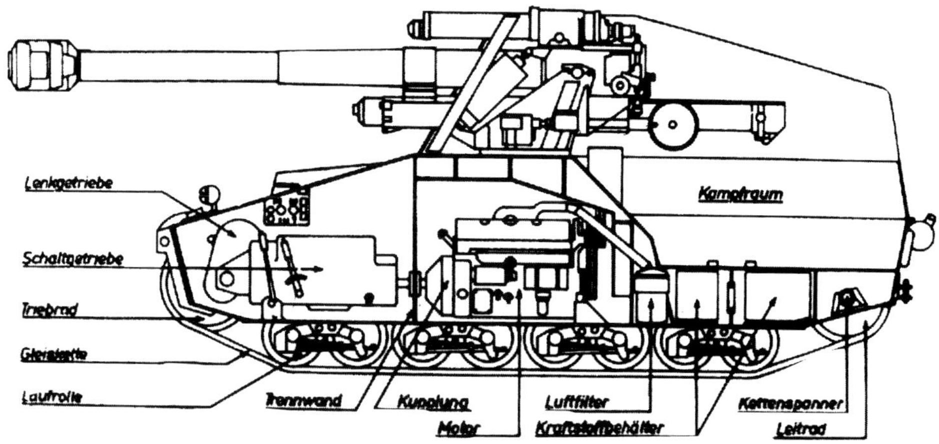

Cutaway drawing of the 15 cm Heavy Howitzer 18 on armored self-propelled Mount IV, taken from the Textbook for Driver Training of Instructional Staff T of Artillery School II, Jüterbog (as of February 1943).

- In defensive combat the gun should be demountable, to afford a smaller target; also, the mount could then be serviced, which was only slightly possible in firing position.
- The self-propelled mounts of the armored artillery fulfill tasks of the artillery and not of the†assault guns, thus splinter and SmK protection was considered sufficient.
- The weight reduction should make for greater mobility.
- An ammunition vehicle similar to the self-propelled artillery mount was to be planned; if the gun car was knocked out, it should be able to take over that vehicle's tasks.

The development of self-propelled artillery mounts that met all these requirements took up much time. Indicative of the progress of the work on these vehicle projects is a notice from the Reich Minister of Armament and War Production, Albert Speer, on the armaments conference with Hitler on July 23-25, 1942:

"Since the Light Howitzer 43 (on self-propelled mount) is a completely new design, three 1:1 scale wooden mockups should be

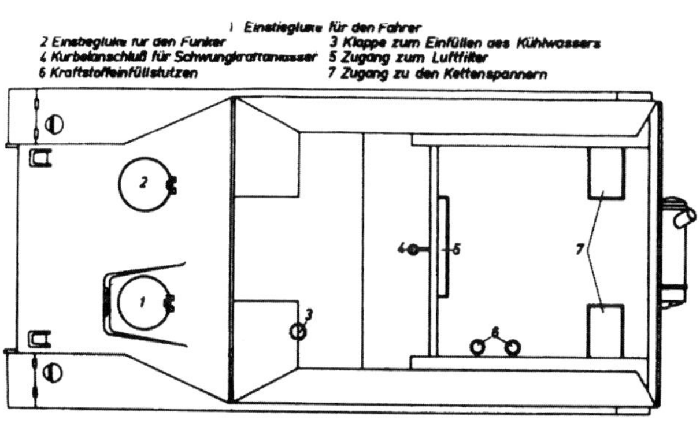

Top view of the 15 cm Heavy Howitzer 18 on armored self-propelled Mount IV (as of February 1943).

produced quickly and developed until the first test gun (April 1, 1943)...."

The Friedrich Krupp AG developed the "Grille" (Cricket) series, which was planned for the 10.5 cm light howitzer, the 15 cm heavy howitzer, and a 12.8 cm cannon then being developed. The Rheinmetall-Borsig GmbH was developing a very similar series of vehicles under the name of†"Scorpion." It could be seen that these self-propelled artillery mounts would not yet be available for the offensive operations in the spring and summer of 1943. To be able to meet the urgent need of the armored artillery for such vehicles temporary solutions were required,

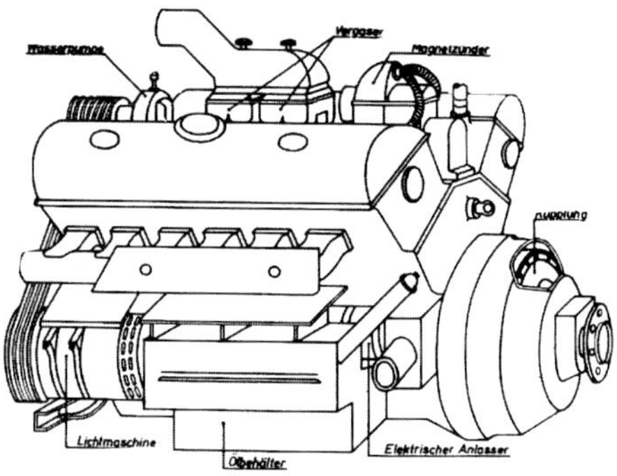

The engine for the armored self-propelled Mount IV, later designated Gun Car III/IV TRM, was the Maybach HL 120 TRM (shown from the right side), which produced 300 HP at 3000 rpm.

The 15 cm armored howitzer bore various designations in its time of troop use. The picture shows such a vehicle used by the Artillery Instructional Unit in the spring of 1943.

to be made by utilizing components from tanks already in production. These included the Panzer II (2cm)(Sd.Kfz.121). On May 13, 1942, Hitler had noted that about 50 of these tanks were being produced per month. Because of its doubtful combat value he gave the notice from the Reich Minister of Armament and War Production, Albert Speer, on the armaments conference with Hitler on July 23-25, 1942:

"Since the Light Howitzer 43 (on self-propelled mount) is a completely new design, three 1:1 scale wooden mockups should be

Future projects for the armored artillery: The 12.8 cm Cannon 43 of the Friedrich Krupp AG on a chassis that was based on components of the Panzer V "Panther" tank (Sd.Kfz.171). With the 12.8 cm cannon it bore the device number 5-1211, with the 15 cm heavy howitzer 5-1228.

Heavy guns on armored self-propelled mounts were also to be put to good use by the Army artillery. A Device 809 with the 17 cm Cannon 44 and a Device 810 with the 21 cm Mortar 18/1 were planned. Only wooden mockups or half-finished prototypes were built.

From the F. Krupp AG of Essen came a suggestion involving a demountable 10.5 cm light howitzer on a lengthened chassis of the Panzer II tank (2 cm)(Sd.Kfz.121).

In 1940 only three prototypes of the Gun Car IV b weapons carrier with 10.5 cm Light Howitzer 18/1 "Heuschrecke" (Grasshopper) 10, were built. The developer was the F. Krupp AG of Essen. The 23-ton vehicle bore 10- to 30-mm armor; the turret and gun could be demounted.

produced quickly and developed until the first test gun (April 1, 1943)...."

The Friedrich Krupp AG developed the "Grille" (Cricket) series, which was planned for the 10.5 cm light howitzer, the 15 cm heavy howitzer, and a 12.8 cm cannon then being developed. The Rheinmetall-Borsig GmbH was developing a very similar series of vehicles under the name of†"Scorpion." It could be seen that these self-propelled artillery mounts would not yet be available for the offensive operations in the spring and summer of 1943. To be able to meet the urgent need of the armored artillery for such vehicles temporary solutions were required, to be made by utilizing components from tanks already in production. These included the Panzer II (2cm)(Sd.Kfz.121). On May 13, 1942, Hitler had noted that about 50 of these tanks were being produced per month. Because of its doubtful combat value he gave the order to find out whether there was still a need for this vehicle among the troops, and whether it might not be more purposeful to produce self-propelled mounts instead.

At the end of July 1942 the chassis of the Panzer II (2cm) tank (Sd.Kfz.121) was chosen as the carrier vehicle for a self-propelled artillery mount with the 10.5 cm Light Howitzer 18 (temporary solution). The Altmärkische Kettenfabrik firm of Borsigwalde received a contract to develop, in a very short time, an armored howitzer out of available gun and vehicle components. After Hitler was shown the results of this developmental work he estimated early in February 1943:

"The light self-propelled mount with the light howitzer on the Panzer II was a very good solution."

Panzer II production was soon to be raised to 100 vehicles per month and used exclusively for self-propelled artillery mounts. In February 1943 the first gun cars with 10.5 cm light howitzers left the FAMO works in Breslau. By June 1944 there were 676 Light Howitzer 18/2 on Panzer II (Sfl.) Chassis (Sd.Kfz.124) in all. The evocative

Final assembly of the 10.5 cm Light Howitzer 18/2 (Sfl.) on Gun Car II (Sd.Kfz. 124) at the Fahrzeug und Motorwnwerke GmbH (FAMO) in Breslau. The self-propelled mount with the evocative name "Wasp" was developed by the Altmärkische Kettenfabrik GmbH (ALKETT) in Berlin-Borsigwalde. In August 1943 57 armored howitzers and 21 ammunition carriers had been delivered.

The 15 cm Heavy Howitzer 18/1 (Sfl.) on Gun Car III/IV, with the evocative name "Hummel" (Bumblebee) (Sd.Kfz. 165), first reached the troops in May 1943. In that year 368 of them were delivered.

The weight of the 15 cm "Hummel" armored howitzer is listed at 24 tons. The armor was 10 to 30 mm thick and offered protection from handgun fire and shell fragments. The crew consisted of six men. Its communications equipment included a type f radio. It carried 18 shells and cartridge cases.

Most of the artillery in the armored and armored grenadier divisions had to make do without armored self-propelled mounts until the war ended.

name "Wespe" (Wasp) was dropped by the Führer's order on February 27, 1944. The self-propelled artillery mounts were joined by 159 self-propelled ammunition carriers. In December 1942 the "Textbook for Driver Training of Light Howitzer 18/II on Armored Self-propelled Mount" had already appeared, published by the Instructional Staff I of Artillery School II, Jüterbog. The D 2020 "Light Howitzer 18/2(Sfl.) on Gw II" dates from May 1, 1943. The Gun Car II was introduced into the two light batteries of the self-propelled units of the armored artillery regiments of armored divisions. Each battery had six Gun Car II (Sd.Kfz. 124) and two Ammunition Carrier II on Sd./Kfz. 124. They proved themselves extraordinarily well in action.

In November 1942 the Krupp-Gruson firm of Magdeburg delivered eight 10.5 cm Light Howitzer 18/1(Sfl.) on Gun Car IV b (Sd.Kfz. 165/1). The gun was housed in a

The C gun of a heavy howitzer battery (mot.) in firing position. To avoid sinking and improve stability, willow mats were placed under the wheels.

The weight of the 10.5 cm "Wespe" armored howitzer is listed as 11 tons. The armor was 8 to 30 mm thick and gave protection from handgun fire and shell fragments. The five-man crew had a type f radio. Thirty-two shells and cartridge cases were carried.

This picture, from the early years of World War II, shows (at right) a light armored observation car (Sd.Kfz.253). Armored observers had to be at the front of attacking units to be able to do their job of directing the batteries' fire.

Repair work on a light armored observation car (Sd.Kfz.253) of the artillery regiment (mot.) of the 21st Armored Division. According to the tactical symbol the vehicle belonged to the 5th Battery of the II. (Light) Unit of the regiment.

At top speed the light armored observation car (Sd.Kfz.252) reached a speed of 60 kph. This picture from North Africa shows a car of the 3rd Battery of the I. (Light) Unit of Artillery Regiment (mot.) 155. This unit belonged to the 21st Armored Division.

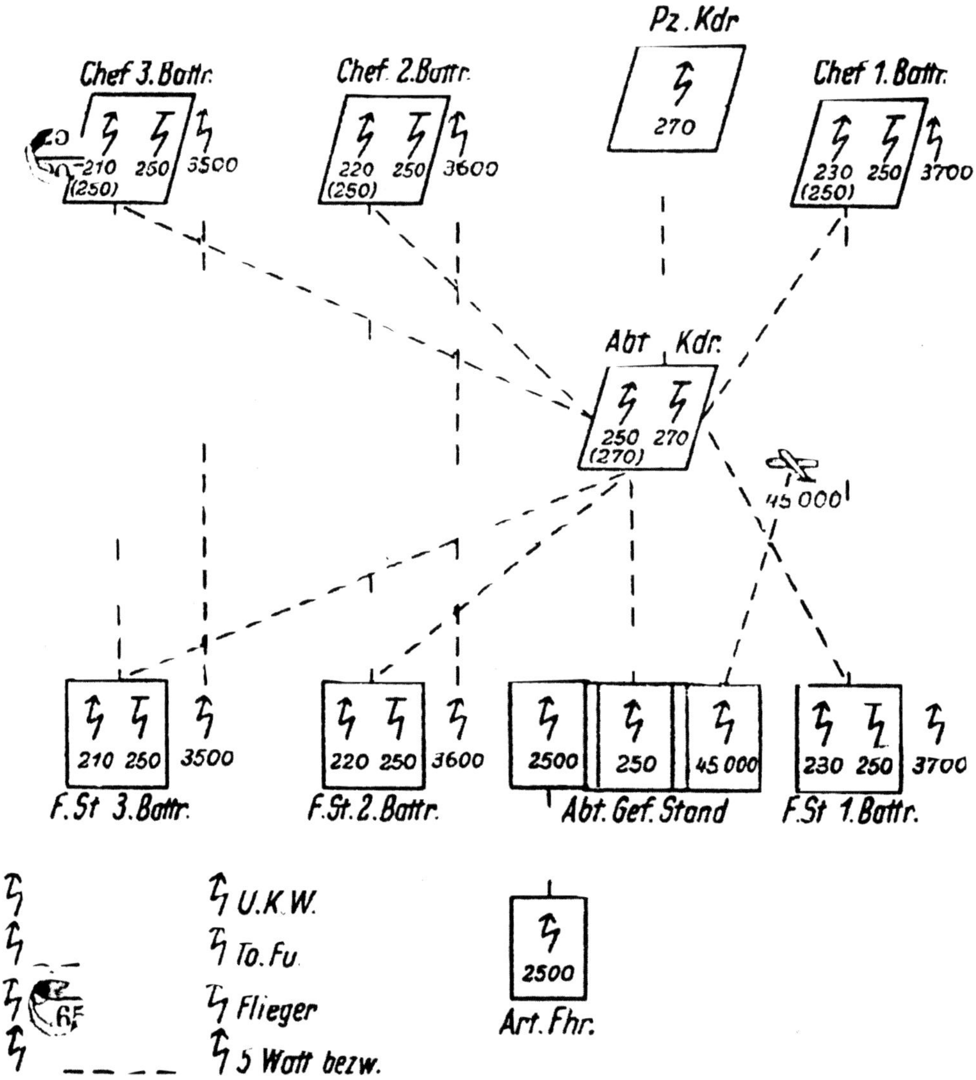

Schematic sketch of the radio and UKW radio links of an armored artillery regiment for a tank attack.

The numbers in parentheses mean that this frequency can be used and heard after switching. The action of the other radio and canister radio troops of the regiment, units, and batteries also used this setup.

turret with a traverse of 70 degrees on the shortened Panzer IV chassis. At the beginning of the month Hitler had decided to stop with this small number. The vehicles did not meet the requirements.

In striving for the final solution of a self-propelled artillery mount with all-around firing ability and a demountable gun, the 105 cm Light Howitzer 1 on Weapons Carrier Gun Car b "Heuschrecke 10" (Grasshopper), made by the Friedrich Krupp AG, was also to be evaluated. The improved 10.5 cm Light Howitzer 43 was intended for planned series production. This did not take place.

Only the three test vehicles delivered and tested in 1943 were built. The same fate was shared by the Light Armored Howitzer 18/40/02 on Gun Car III/IV(Sfl.). One prototype was built. There is an explanation for this cancellation: The production capacity for Panzer IV chassis was urgently needed for producing pursuit tanks and assault guns. Besides, the Gun Car II (Sd.Kfz. 124), using the 10.5 cm Light Howitzer 18, met the troops' requirements.

Let us turn now to the self-propelled artillery mount with the 15 cm Heavy Howitzer 18. Here, too, a temporary solution was sought. In any case, only wooden mockups of the final solutions being developed were ever made. The Altmärkische Kettenfabrik of Borsigwalde once again received a developmental contract. From Speer's notes—already quoted several times—about the armament conference with Hitler on July 23-25, 1942, it is seen that the self-propelled mount with the 15 cm heavy howitzer was also only a temporary solution. It remained in production, though, until the war ended. On October 6, 1942, Adolf Hitler, Reich Chancellor and Commander of the Wehrmacht, was shown the iron model of a self-propelled mount, using the same components, for the 8.8 cm Tank-destroyer Cannon 43 ("Hornisse" = Hornet), and for

This picture shows one of the ten 15 cm "Hummel" armored howitzers (Sd.Kfz.165) made by modifying other tank chassis. Disadvantages of the self-propelled mounts included steering errors and location difficulties. Handling the heavy vehicle was not easy in mud or very cold weather.

A dug-in light armored observation car (Sd.Kfz.253) of the armored artillery, seen in 1943. These striking vehicles were quickly spotted by the enemy and taken under fire.

the 15 cm Heavy Howitzer 18 ("Hummel" = Bumblebee). He was very pleased with the developments and awaited the advent of the planned production of 100 vehicles each by May 12, 1943. The carrier vehicle was a combination of components and parts from the Panzer III and IV tanks, designated Gun Car III/IV. As with Gun Car II, the engine was in the middle of the vehicle. The following uses were suggested by the Altmärkische Kettenfabrik:

Device 804 Gun Car III/IV for 10.5 cm Light Howitzer 18/40/2 (Sfl.)
Device 807 Gun Car III/IV for 15 cm Heavy Howitzer 181(Sfl.)
Device 812 Gun Car III/IV for 15 cm Heavy Howitzer 18/5(Sfl.)

Only Device 807 was produced and introduced to the troops as the 15 cm Heavy Howitzer 18/1 on Gun Car III/IV (Sd.Kfz.165). The much better-known nickname "Hummel" was dropped, at least officially, at the beginning of 1944. The Instructional Staff T of the Artillery School II in Jüterbog put out the "Textbook for Driver Training, Heavy Field Howitzer 18 on Armored Self-propelled Mount IV" in February 1943. Such publications helped to acquaint the armored artillerymen quickly with the new technology and assure its usefulness in the realm of their own planned attack operations in the east. Note the very different designation for the self-propelled mount. In all, 724 15 cm armored howitzers (including ten made by modifying other chassis) were produced. There were also 157 ammunition carriers on the Sd.Kfz.165. Six 15 cm Heavy Howitzer 18/1 on Gun Car III/IV(Sfl.)(Sd.Kfz.165) and two ammunition carriers belonged to a heavy battery of the self-propelled gun units in the armored artillery regiments of the armored divisions. Although designated only as makeshift or temporary solutions, without the required all-

Within one year (April 1943 to April 1944) 262 Armored Scout Car III (Sd.Kfz.143) were built. The vehicles intended for the armored howitzer batteries included two Armored Scout Car III (Sd.Kfz.143) and one fire-control Schützenpanzerwagen (Sd.Kfz.251/3) with the same radio equipment. The manufacturing of a medium armored scout car (Sd.Kfz. 251/18) began only in August 1944.

The turret of the Armored Scout Car III (Sd.Kfz.143) from the collection of the Military Technical Museum in Koblenz. The port with the ball mantlet for a Machine Gun 34 and the armored peephole for the observation telescope are easy to see.

In the intelligence platoons of the batteries (mot.) of the armored artillery regiments (mot.) there were, besides an armored scout car (Sd.Kfz.253 or 254), three radio cars (Kfz.15 or 17). The unarmored vehicles needed a particularly effective camouflage, as can be seen here, to protect them from enemy weapons.

around firing ability for the gun, and without the desired high degree of mobility, superior to that of a tank, these vehicles proved themselves well in action.

The equipping of at least one unit of the armored artillery regiments with self-propelled guns, begun in the early summer of 1943, also placed new demands on the armored vehicles needed for the command and observation of artillery combat. Because of the uniqueness of their use high mobility was required. The new type of Panzer II tank then being developed came closest to equaling it. The VK 903 Armored Scout Car was based on it. It carried a three-man crew and reached a speed of 65 kph. The specially designed turret had a range finder and extensive radio equipment. To bridge the gap to planned series production of the VK 903, the Armored Scout Car III (Sd.Kfz.143) was introduced. The Device Description (D 652/

The light armored scout car (Sd.Kfz.253), like the light Schützenpanzerwagen (Sd.Kfz.250), was based on the chassis of the 1-ton Demag D 7 light tractor (Sd.Kfz.11). The 5.7-ton vehicle bore 8- to 18-mm armor. The four-man crew had a Machine Gun 34 for self defense.

The Armored Scout Car III (Sd.Kfz.143) weighed up to 23 tons and achieved mobility comparable to the armored howitzers with a speed of 40 kph. The five-man crew had an assortment of radio and observation devices. The armor was 10 to 80 mm thick. Note the dummy cannon on the turret.

27) appeared on April 23, 1943. Between February 1943 and April 1944 262 of them were built. In terms of radio technology, it was already equipped like the final version, the Vk 903. This included:

- one 30-watt medium-wave transmitter and receiver (Fu 8),
- one medium-wave receiver (Fu 4),
- one Type f radio device,
- the on-board speaker system,
- one Type g canister radio (intended for use outside the scout car).

The armored scout car was also equipped with a periscope. The first vehicles of this type had no big gun; in its place was a dummy. Later the Armored Scout Car III (Sd.Kfz.143) was delivered with a 5 cm Kampfwagenkanone 39 L/60. Then came 90 Armored Scout Car IV that had to be adapted from the steady production of Panzer IV tanks (7.5 cm)(Sd.Kfz.161/2) between July 1944 and March 1945, and 41 Armored Scout Car V†"Panther."

The armored artillery regiments of the armored divisions, which were combined for the "Operation Citadel" offensive in July 1943, had priority on armored howitzers and armored scout cars, which reached the troops beginning in May. The II. Unit, Armored Artillery Regiment 103 (4th Armored Division), received six "Wespen" each for its 4th and 5th Batteries and six "Hummeln" for its 6th Battery early in July. Seven Armored Scout Car III (Sd.Kfz.143) also were sent, of which two went to the regimental staff and five to the II. Unit. Each battery got one Armored Scout Car III (Sd.Kfz.143) and one light or medium Armored Observation Car (Sd.Kfz.250/5 or 251/5); two Armored Scout Car III (Sd.Kfz.143) and one Medium Armored Observation Car (Sd.Kfz.251/5) belonged to

In the heavy howitzer batteries of the artillery units (mot.) in the armored and armored grenadier divisions, the standard of four guns was retained to war's end. The picture shows a 15 cm Heavy Howitzer 18 (mot.) battery in firing position.

These 15 cm Heavy Howitzer 18 (mot.) are being prepared for direct firing. For antitank use, in which a high final velocity of the shell, a flat trajectory, a large danger zone, and a short flight time are advantageous, the 6th charge, delivered ready to fire, was used.

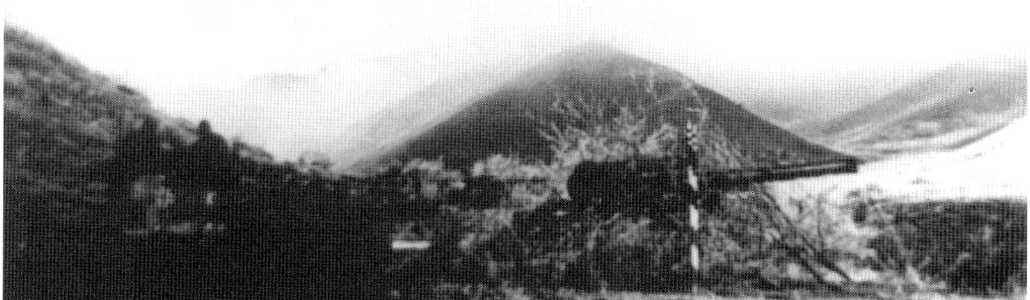

Howitzers of the III. (heavy) Unit, Armored Artillery Regiment 13 of the 13th Armored Division are in covered positions. At left is an armored observation vehicle (Sd.Kfz.253. The picture was taken during the withdrawal fighting in the Caucasus early in 1943.

Advantages of the armored self-propelled mounts in the armored howitzer units of the armored artillery regiments were their greater tactical mobility, armor protection, and quicker readiness to fire. In the picture is a 10.5 cm Light Howitzer 18/2 (Sfl.) on Gun Car II "Wespe" (Sd.Kfz.124) in firing position.

The five-man crew of Armored Scout Car III (Sd.Kfz.143) consisted of the observer, assistant observer, driver, and two radiomen. For observation, and while the armored howitzer batteries were firing, the armored scout cars had to stop.

the staff battery of the self-propelled gun unit. The other two units (I. and III.), made mobile for motorized marches, were each supplied with five light or medium Armored Observation Cars (Sd.Kfz.250/5 or 251/5).

From September 1944 on, the self-propelled gun units were generally the first units of the armored artillery regiments. The war formation planned on the following numbers of guns:

- Twelve 10.5 cm Light Howitzer 18.18 or 18/40 (mot.Z.),
- Twelve 10.5 cm Light Howitzer 18/1 (Sfl.),
- Eight 15 cm Heavy Howitzer 18 (mot.Z.),
- Six 15 cm Heavy Howitzer [p. 107] 18/1 (Sfl.),
- Four 10 cm Heavy Cannon 18 (mot.Z.).

A light armored howitzer battery in firing position. From the start, the structure of such a battery included six guns.

Towing vehicles and guns of a heavy howitzer battery (mot.) pass a horsedrawn unit. Unpaved roads were not to be used by the heavy towed units if possible. During the mud season in particular, they very often got stuck and were useless for long periods.

An 8-ton Medium Towing Tractor KM m 11 (Sd.Kfz.7) tows a 10 cm Heavy Cannon 18 on the march. In mid-October 1943 Hitler had ordered increased production of this gun type. The production of the tractor type needed for them was also to be increased. In 1943, 454 10 cm Heavy Cannon 18 were delivered. They were not enough to replace the lost guns.

The numerous deviations from the planned numbers, which were found, especially after the autumn of 1943, can be noted here only through individual examples. Various armored artillery regiments consisted only of two units, while Armored Artillery Regiments 155 (21st Armored Division) and 91 (25th Armored Division) lacked armored observation batteries. These were taken from the armored artillery regiments in any case by the end of 1943. Some artillery units used foreign guns, including Russian 12.2 cm howitzers.

While the bulk of the eleven armored grenadier divisions had no self-propelled guns in their artillery regiments (mot.), there were exceptions here, too. The artillery regiments (mot.) of the 90th Armored Grenadier Division had two batteries with "Wespen". In the 3rd and 29th Armored Grenadier Divisions there were also self-propelled guns, and in the "Grossdeutschland" Armored Grenadier Division, whose artillery regiment had four units, including one with self-propelled guns. The "Brandenburg" and "Feldherrnhalle" Armored Grenadier Divisions, established in 1944, officially each had an armored artillery regiment with a unit of self-propelled guns. It becomes clear that the introduction of self-propelled artillery mounts in the armored artillery resulted in extensive changes in their structure and organization. The effects on tactics will be portrayed in the following chapter.

Work continued to be done on the development of self-propelled artillery mounts. Not very promising in terms of armament economy were weapons carriers that were to be built with components of the Panzer V "Panther," or other newly developed or proposed tank designs. There were models, and in some cases cast steel prototypes of them. This was also true of the 17 cm cannon (Sfl.) and the 21 cm mortar (Sfl.), self-propelled guns that were projected and developed for use by the army artillery. The project to build a light and a heavy armored howitzer on Gun Car III/IV, which was planned for the Stahlindustrie AG firm with 45 and 25 vehicles to be built per month, came to an early end—production began in May 1945! A more realistic proposal was made in September 1943 to mount the 10.5 cm Light Howitzer 18/40 removably on the 3-ton light towing tractor (Sd.Kfz.11). Tests in this direction continued until the war ended. At the beginning of 1945 the Hanomag firm of Hannover delivered six self-propelled 10.5 cm Light Howitzer 18/40 on Type D Medium Schützenpanzerwagen (Sd.Kfz.251) to Artillery Regiment 33 (mot.) of the 15th Armored Grenadier Division. The gun could be removed with a 2-ton makeshift crane and set onto the wheeled mount that accompanied it. Thus, at least the request for a demountable gun made in 1942 was fulfilled. This vehicle more or less marks the end of development of self-propelled artillery mounts in Germany during World War II. It was a modest end to high-flying plans and projects.

Units of a heavy 10 cm cannon battery (mot.) are on the march to a new firing position. Because of the guns' great range, the delaying of enemy reserves' approach and development ranked among these batteries' tasks.

VI. TACTICAL PROBLEMS OF THE ARMORED ARTILLERY 1943-1945

Basically, self-propelled gun batteries had six guns instead of the usual four. Vehicle breakdowns on the march were not supposed to affect artillery firepower. Batteries thus equipped were able to follow the fast-developing combat action of the tanks and armored grenadiers (gp.) closely and quickly. Artillery on self-propelled mounts had the advantage of being less sensitive to enemy infantry and artillery firepower than the guns towed by motor vehicles. In H.Dv. 298/3a "Training prerequisites for the armored troops, command and combat of the armored grenadiers, Volume I The Armored Grenadier Battalion (gp.)" of August 5, 1944, it is further stated:

"Speed, offroad capability and plentiful equipment with intelligence devices allow the armored artillery quick readiness to fire and enable them to support the combat of the armored grenadiers (gp.) decisively. Hereby the self-propelled artillery also has the advantage of quick mobility. Their disadvantages, though, are their meager supply of ammunition and the loss of the gun if the self-propelled mount breaks down."

In long combat duration this became a serious problem, for the two ammunition carriers that were set up to take up the guns were not available for unlimited durations. When they were used as gun cars the

Vehicles of an armored battle group on the march. Armored self-propelled guns were particularly suited for cooperation with tanks and armored grenadiers on Schützenpanzerwagen.

In August 1943 40 "Hummel" armored howitzers (Sd.Kfz.165) were delivered. The monthly production was sufficient to equip six armored howitzer batteries.

ammunition supply in the gun units, not generous to begin with, was decreased. The 3-ton trucks available in the supply units of the staff batteries were often not sufficiently offroad-capable to bring spare ammunition to the gun crews. A further problem occurred. There was often a lack of recovery vehicles, in this case the 189-ton heavy towing tractor (Sd.Kfz.9). If one self-propelled gun broke down from mechanical damage, that usually meant the loss of a second vehicle, which was the self-propelled gun used to tow the damaged vehicle away. In action, especially on the eastern front, it was seen how justified the armored artillery's request for full all-around firing ability by the self-propelled guns was. The meager traverse of the howitzers on the Gun Car II (20 degrees) and III/IV (15 degrees) often made turning the entire vehicle necessary. In mud and very cold weather, major turns were†"not always simple." Inability to turn and locate targets were the fatal results of the armored artillery's dependence on speed and precision in combat.

The war experiences showed clearly the growing importance of the artillery in terms of offensive and defensive combat. Armored artillery units with self-propelled guns, armored grenadier battalions (gp.), and tank units were among the most important components of the armored battle groups. It was the armored artillery's job to fight against such targets as could be attacked by the weapons of tanks and armored grenadiers (gp.) only with insufficient effect. These were targets in low spots, on the†"wide flanks," and†very extended and resistant targets. In such cases the artillery fire had to be concentrated quickly, a task of the armored artillery commanders and observers who, in their armored scout cars, accompanied the action of tanks and armored grenadiers on their Schützenpanzerwagen. Armored scout cars had always been the problem children. Their striking appearance and many antennae made it easy to spot them in an attacking pack of tanks and shoot them down. The artillery's armored scout cars, which supported the attacks of tanks and armored grenadiers more or less directly, had to take their places as far forward as possible before the attack began. That made target spotting and fire control easier; short connections allowed quick action against targets. Their distribution and UKW radio positions required anticipatory command. Personal voice contact among the leaders of all the involved tanks and artillery made combat command easier. The place of the artillery leader of an armored division on the march and in combat was near the battle-group commander, who led the mass of the armored artillery. If a unit (as a rule, the self-propelled unit) was ordered to cooperate with the tanks, the unit commander in his Armored Scout Car III (Sd.Kfz.143) accompanied the tank attack in order to have a constant view of the combat terrain. Only then was he able to direct the supporting fire of his unit.

As a rule, the artillery fired from covered firing positions. Thus, direct aiming possibilities for short-range defense against approaching enemy tanks had to be determined and prepared. The following tasks could be given to the armored artillery regiment of an armored division:

1. Before the tank attack (from the readiness position):

- Shooting down recognized enemy artillery that was able to affect the area of the tank attack with destructive fire, or in cooperation with artillery aviators and the armored observation battery (if available or assigned);

Four 15 cm Howitzer 18 (mot.) of a howitzer battery are in firing position. Before the firing began, the battery leader had to order the basic direction. It was the basis for the traversing ability of the whole battery, and also of the effectiveness of their use.

In D 2020 "Light Howitzer 18/2 (Sfl.) on Gw II, Description" of May 1 1943 the self-propelled mount was described thoroughly. Its uses were seen as fighting living targets and covered positions with explosive shells. The 10.5 cm Light Howitzer 18/2 (Sfl) could not be fired without a muzzle brake.

At first, unchanged chassis of the Panzer II (2 cm) (Sd.Kfz.121) were used for the gun Car II. Vehicles produced later were recognizable by their leading wheels placed farther back. The last pair of wheels had additional springs.

- Destructive fire on recognized enemy tank groups;
- Fire attacks on areas in which antitank weapons are spotted or can be suspected. Focal points are areas in which the tanks themselves cannot have an effect, but from which they are endangered;
- Zeroing in, with explosive shells with impact fuzes, on known or suspected enemy observation points that overlook the attack routes and could have smoke laid as your own attack begins;

2. During the tank attack:

- Attacking enemy antitank defense, above all outside the attack route and as your own tanks advance into the depth of the defenses;
- Blinding the enemy observation points;
- Keeping down the enemy artillery;
- Keeping down the enemy infantry and their rearward parts on the front and the flanks.

Also, as long as positions allow, covering your own tank attack through the use of fog ammunition;

- Delaying the approach and development of enemy reserves (especially of tank forces) at long distances.

The participation of units directly involved in tank support in the artillery preparation before the attack was dependent on ammunition supplies. For pursuit after a successful breakthrough into enemy-free territory, the self-propelled gun unit was particularly suited. It followed the tanks, using all means of staying close behind the armored battle group, or at its last stopping point, in order to be able to go into position immediately in case of renewed enemy opposition. If the armored battle group fought with open flanks (which was the rule), then the armored artillery had to secure the firing positions carefully, so as to be protected from surprise attacks.

Assembly of the Gun Car III/IV was carried out by the Deutsche Eisenwerke of Duisburg. The armor came from the Deutsche Röhrenwerke of Mühlheim.

In the collection of the Wehrtechnische Museum in Koblenz is this 10.5 cm Light Howitzer 18/2 (Sfl.) on a Gun Car II "Wespe" (Sd/Kfz.124). The breech of the gun is stamped with csf 42, indicating the manufacturer and year of manufacture (Wittenauer Maschinenfabrik GmbH, Berlin-Borsigwalde, Flohrstrasse, 1942). The manufacturer of the gun car was the Fahrzeug†und Motorenwerke GmbH of Breslau and Warsaw (formerly Ursus).

Further units of the 10.5 cm Light Howitzer 18/2 (Sfl.) on Gun Car II "Wespe" (Sd.Kfz.124). The mount carries the gun and aims it with the help of the elevation and traverse controls.

The unarmored tractors were especially sensitive to artillery fire and air attacks. There were 3251 8-ton medium tractors made in 1943, and 3298 in 1944. In spite of that, their numbers were not enough to replace all losses.

The two units of the armored artillery regiments that were equipped with towing tractors and 10.5 cm Light and 15 cm Heavy Howitzer 18 and 10 cm Heavy Cannon 18 had to accompany tank attacks with fire directed by their advanced observers, and then make position changes to the front. Disadvantages were the meager range of the howitzers and the insufficient effect of 10 cm heavy cannon shells. To be sure, the towing tractors allowed greater operative mobility, an advantage that lost importance in the battles of 1944-45. The lack of armor protection made these parts of the armored artillery regiments sensitive to fire, as was learned in earlier war years. They were also threatened by fighter and bomber planes that ruled the air space over the German forces.

On September 13, 1944, Handbook 80/1 "Guidelines for Cooperation Between Tanks and Artillery" was published. It is noteworthy that the Inspector General of the Armored Troops and the General of the Artillery in the Army General Staff appeared equally as authors. The guidelines dealt primarily with the combat and cooperation of tanks and artillery in the infantry divisions. For cooperation of tanks and artillery in the armored divisions, the principles set forth in Artillery Handbook No. 25, "Temporary Guidelines for Use and Action of Artillery in Armored Divisions," issued on October 9, 1942, remained valid. Thus, Handbook 80/1 would not need to be considered in this portrayal of the development of the armored artillery if changed focal points in the combat of armored troops were not reflected in them. The great era of the tank attack was over. It was already difficult to assemble battle-ready armored groups for†"firemen's actions," which would have been effective in cleaning up critical situations at the front. The main

Front and rear views of the 15 cm Heavy Howitzer 18/1 (Sfl.) on Gun Car III/IV "Hummel" (Sd.Kfz.165), from the collection of the Military Technical Museum in Koblenz.

According to a request of May 1943, some 100 "Hummel" armored howitzers (Sd.Kfz.165) were to be prepared for the offensive operations in the summer of 1943. In June of that year 85 of them were with the troops. That was how many twelve armored divisions were supposed to have.

157 of the "Hummel" self-propelled ammunition carrier, also called Gun Car III/IV (Mun.), were delivered. They could carry 90 shells and cartridge cases. Every armored howitzer battery had two vehicles of this type.

tank of the decimated tank forces was to give the infantry "corset-bone" strength and defensive power. It is also stated in Handbook 80/1:

"Tanks and artillery have the task of supporting the infantry in their hard fighting. Attacks and counterattacks of tanks to support the infantry against defense-ready enemies require sufficient fire protection from the artillery."

Armored artillery, trained and experienced in cooperation with tanks, was seldom available to carry out such tasks. The tank companies and platoons subordinate to the infantry commanders had to cooperate with the horsedrawn artillery in the infantry divisions. Guderian had concluded as much in his prewar writings; now necessity had made it a daily practice.

This noteworthy picture from 1943 shows the results of a battle between a 10.5 cm Light Howitzer 18 (mot.) and a Russian 1943 model T-34 tank. In battle against attacking tanks this type of gun had little chance for success. It could hit targets with direct fire at ranges under 500 meters. The meager rate of fire (6 rounds per minute) was a disadvantage, but the strong effect of the 10.5 cm antitank or hollow-charge shell in direct hits was an advantage.

Here a damaged 3-ton Opel Blitz 3.6-6700A medium offroad-capable truck of the ammunition troop of a motorized howitzer battery is being towed to the repair shop.

The drivers of an ammunition troop pose proudly with a 15 cm Granate 19 FES shell with 23 umg. (0.15) contact fuze. In the last two war years problems with ammunition supply were an everyday occurrence. Their solution was decisive for the efficiency of attacks, including those of the armored artillery.

Endless columns of vehicles were the sensitive arteries of the Army's armored units. This picture was taken in July 1943 during Operation "Citadel" at the Kursk bend.

Three-ton HL kl 6 Light Tractors (Sd.Kfz.11) of a motorized light howitzer battery are seen on the march. In 1943, 2153 vehicles of this type were produced, and in 1944 only 1308.

This 8-ton KM m 11 Medium Tractor (Sd.Kfz.7) towing a 15 cm Heavy Howitzer 18 (mot.) has gotten stuck while fording a river. Every battery had another tractor of this type available for recovery; it could also be used as a replacement towing tractor.

These pictures show the action of a 10.5 cm "Wespe" armored howitzer (Sd.Kfz.124) battery during the combat in the Kursk bend in July 1943. The armored howitzers have already taken firing positions. In the background, a 10.5 cm Light Howitzer 18 (mot.) is seen being unloaded. To the right of the firing positions, two "Wespe" self-propelled ammunition carriers are arriving.

In the center of the picture, a "Wespe" self-propelled ammunition carrier, or Gun Car II (Mun.), can be seen. From February 1943 to July 1944 159 of them were produced. One vehicle could transport 90 shells and cartridge cases.

Members of an armored howitzer battery are eating their lunch. A cartridge box serves as a table, with shell baskets for the light howitzers serving as chairs. In the background are shell boxes for 10 cm Hl/Z shells.

The five-man crew of a 10.5 cm Light Howitzer 18/2 (Sfl.) on Gun Car II "Hummel" (Sd./Kfz.124) enjoy a firing pause during the battles of July 1943.

A fully camouflaged 10.5 cm Light Howitzer 18/2 (Sfl.) on Gun Car II "Wespe" (Sd.Kfz.124) in firing position. Concealing the valuable vehlcies on the battlefield was a high priority.

This 10.5 cm Light Howitzer 19/2 (Sfl.) on Gun Car II "Wespe" (Sd.Kfz.124) has ruined its barrel. The life span of a howitzer barrel was stated as 8000 to 10,000 rounds.

A material attack is shown during Operation "Citadel" in July 1943. At right is an armored fire control car (Sd.Kfz.251/3) of a light armored howitzer battery.

This crew of a 10.5 cm "Wespe" armored howitzer (Sd.Kfz.124) was photographed in 1943.

Armored howitzers withdraw across the Dniepr on a pontoon ferry moved by a powerboat.

VII. STRUCTURE AND MATERIALS OF THE ARMORED ARTILLERY IN THE LAST TWO WAR YEARS

At the end of 1942 the field army had fewer light howitzers than during the French campaign. In addition, the numbers of worn out barrels had grown considerably.

The monthly production simply was not enough to fill the existing holes. In March 1942 44 10.5 cm Light Howitzer 18 were received. In mid-May 1943 Hitler ordered a rise in monthly production to 800 guns of this type. At that time just 337 of them were produced. Only a year later, in May 1944, could Hitler's order be filled: 805 10.5 cm Light Howitzer 18M and 18/40 were delivered. During 1943 the number of light howitzers in the field army rose again, as 4101 newly made guns outbalanced 3075 losses. In June 1944 the number reached 8060, but by that November it sank to 6842. A very different development was seen with the 15 cm Heavy Howitzer 18. Its numbers had decreased constantly since 1941. A monthly average of 82 guns in 1942-43 and 93 on 1943-44 ranked as total losses. Planning in May 1943 called for monthly production to be raised to 200 heavy howitzers, a goal that could be attained only through extreme efforts, so†the numbers grew slowly. In June 1944 there were 2878 of them with the field army, and five months later only 2629.

In 1942 there were, on average, somewhat more than 100 of the 10 cm Heavy Cannon

This 15 cm Heavy Howitzer 18/1 (Sfl.) on Gun Car III/IV belonged to the 3rd (heavy) battery of the armored howitzer unit of an armored artillery regiment. This battery had six heavy armored howitzers and two self-propelled ammunition carriers.

Beginning in 1940 the improved 10.5 cm Light Howitzer 18 M was delivered to the troops. The letter M indicates the muzzle brake with which the gun was equipped. Six different charges and a special ready-to-fire long-distance charge were available for firing. With the last, Fern howitzer shells (Vnull 540 m/s) could be fired up to 12,325 meters.

18 in the field army. In October 1942 the order came from Hitler to increase the monthly production of these guns. Another increase came in March 1943; 75 were requested, without great success. The yearly production for 1943 was just enough to equal the losses. In June 1944 there were 325 of the 10 cm Heavy Cannon 18 in the field army, a number that decreased to 233 by November of that year.

This comparison of the changing numbers of important field guns in the German Army, also of great importance for the armored artillery, shows what difficulties arose in equalizing the great losses of the eastern campaign's first year. Negative developmental trends remained in the combat strength of the field army. Their firepower, and thus their fighting power, decreased constantly at a time when the armored artillery was expected to make up for the decreased offensive and defensive power of the tanks and armored grenadiers. For example, Armored Artillery Regiment 89 (24th Armored Division) reported, early in April 1944, the possession of five armored howitzers, seven 15 cm Heavy Howitzer 18 (mot.Z.), and four 10 cm Heavy Cannon 18 (mot.Z.). That was exactly 50% of what they should have had. In the period from

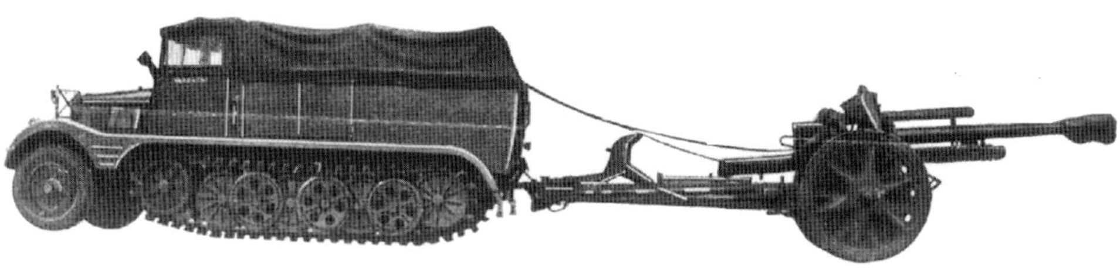

The 3-ton HL kl 6 Light Tractor (Sd.Kfz.11) with a 10.5 cm Light Howitzer 18 M (mot.). In firing position the gun weighed 2065 kilograms.

This 10.5 cm Light Howitzer 18 M (mot.) belongs to the collection of the Military History Museum of Dresden.

A 10.5 cm Light Howitzer 18 M (mot.) in firing position. The barrel with its muzzle brake was 3308 mm long. During the war, spoked wooden wheels with hard rubber tires replaced aluminum or steel disc wheels. This picture was taken on the eastern front in March 1944.

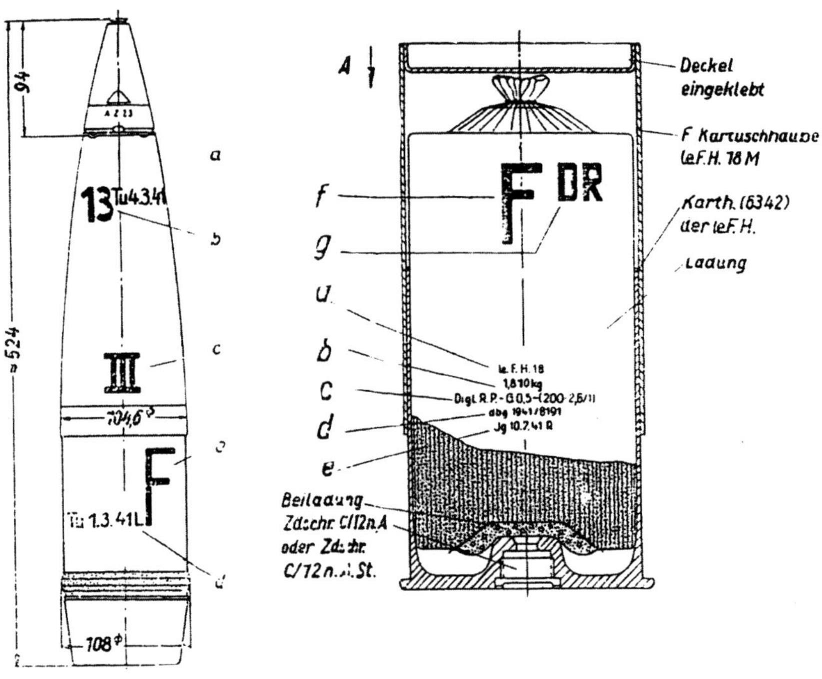

The Fern (long-range) howitzer shell and long-distance cartridge case for the 10.5 cm Light Howitzer 18 M.

December 1, 1943, to November 30, 1944, the armored artillery lost 257 10.5 cm Light Howitzer 18/2 on Panzer II chassis (Sfl.)(Sd.Kfz.124), 240 15 cm Heavy Howitzer 18/1 on Gun Car III/IV (Sfl.)(Sd.Kfz.165), 143 Armored Scout Car III (Sd/Kfz.143), and six Armored Scout Car IV in the eastern theater of war. It was increasingly difficult to replace the losses. On May 1, 1944, it was reported that, because of a delay in engine and gearbox production, first the full number of assault guns was to be produced, and then the production capacities would be available for self-propelled artillery guns. Production of the 10.5 cm armored howitzer was halted in the summer of 1944, and that of the 15 cm armored howitzer at the beginning of 1945. As a result of the growing losses their numbers in the troops were decreasing. Production of the successor model on Gun Car III/IV, made by the Stahlindustrie AG firm, was planned only as of May 1945. In a report of the Army High Command, Organizational Unit III, of April 26, 1945, the monthly production of 180 Weapons Carrier 38 is also mentioned. It was to be equipped with the 10.5 cm Light Howitzer 18/40.

There were only prototypes of these. These few numbers show the whole dilemma that faced military equipment production at that time. On February 23, 1945, the same office had tried to spread optimism with the following report:

The 10.5 cm Light Howitzer 18 M (mot.) of a motorized light artillery unit that saw action with an armored artillery regiment in Italy. It was towed by a 3-ton HL kl 6 Light Tractor (Sd.Kfz.11).

"Within a few months of the beginning of the Russian winter offensive in the east alone, weapons arrived via supply routes as follows:

- Light Howitzers 350
- Heavy Howitzers 190
- 10 cm Heavy Cannon 90"

In firing position, the barrel of the 15 cm heavy howitzer, weighing over 1.7 tons, had to be moved from marching to firing position by a hand crank.. At the same time the leaf springs of the axle were unbolted, so that the mount could adjust to uneven ground.

A 15 cm Heavy Howitzer 18 (mot.) of the 10th Battery, SS Artillery Regiment (mot.)†"Viking," in firing position before Kropotnik on the Kuban, photographed on August 5, 1942. This regiment became SS Armored Artillery Regiment 5 of the SS Armored Division "Viking" in the summer of 1943 (as of October 22, 1943, the 5th SS Armored Division "Viking").

Staff Battery (mot.) of an Artillery Unit (mot.) of an Armored Division, according to War Strength Report No. 583 of November 1, 1943.

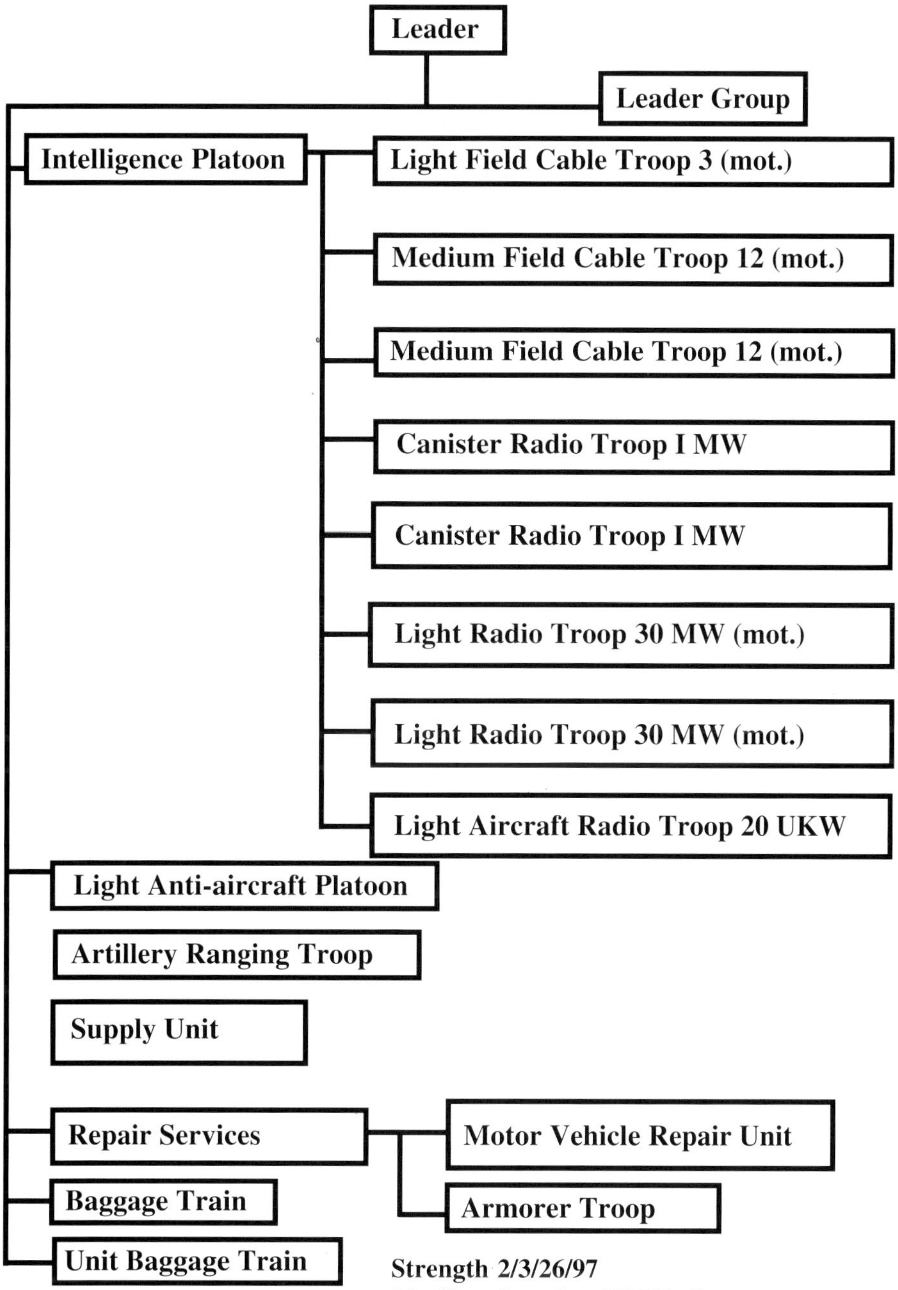

Strength 2/3/26/97
2 halftrack cycles (Sd.Kfz.2)
36 cars and trucks
3 2-cm Mountain Flak 38 guns

Many armored artillery regiments, at least until the autumn of 1943, had their own armored observation batteries. If needed, light observation units (mot.) that belonged to the Army troops could be subordinated to them. They were composed of a staff battery (mot.), a light-measuring battery (mot.) with balloon platoon, and a sound-measuring battery. There were few chances of utilizing the balloon platoons because of the growing threat from enemy fighter planes.

These figures say little about the numerous breakdowns. Armored Artillery Regiment 103 (4th Armored Division) received light howitzers with iron tires early in February 1945, and they had to be exchanged for those with rubber tires. Of the specified number of 14 15 cm heavy howitzers, eight were lacking. Improvement could not be expected. Information on the production of the 10.5 cm Light Howitzer 18/40, 925 of which had been delivered in October 1944, was completely lacking in April 1945 (108 were built in March). For the 15 cm Heavy Howitzer 18, 40 are listed. In October 1944 there were 263, and in March 1945 there were 151.

The great efforts made since 1943 to sustain or even increase the numbers of guns in the divisions of the field army did not lack for negative effects on the further development of artillery armaments. At first there were efforts to modernize the guns. With the introduction of the 10.5 cm Light Howitzer 18 M the range was increased from 10,675 to 12,325 meters. The 10.5 cm Light Howitzer 18/40 came into use as a transitional weapon, reaching the troops in the spring of 1943 using the only slightly modified mount of the 7.5 cm Antitank Cannon 40. As early as late June 1942, Hitler had ordered a considerable range increase for the guns of the divisional artillery. His wish was also that of the troops. In this respect, neither the 10.5 cm Light Howitzer 42 nor the Model 43 then being developed was satisfactory. In spite of that, the decision was made in favor of the latter gun, for which a range of up to 15,000 meters was expected. Besides those built by Rheinmetall-Borsig GmbH, there were others made by the Friedrich Krupp AG and Skoda. The new all-around firing mounts of these guns were noteworthy, and were based on experience gained in the campaigns to date. Until the war ended there were only wooden mockups and a few test models. A switch to series production of the new models during the course of the war became more and more unlikely, for reasons already noted. To make the ranges of the guns in use by the troops equal the superior parameters of the foreign field guns, tests were made with special cartridges and special "extended-range shells." At the beginning of 1945, the Führer's headquarters amazed the Army Weapons Office with the suggestion of switching the entire field artillery from the 10.5 cm light howitzer to a 7.5 cm cannon. At this point six different models had already been presented. The reasons for this very controversial decision were based on the unsolved problem of antitank defense, which was growing into a crisis at the front. The Chief of the Organization Unit in the Army High Command, Generalleutnant Walter Buhle, told the opponents of this decision on February 24, 1945:

"The basic requirement that cannons for antitank defense must be made in the greatest possible numbers and would prove to be correspondingly effective in use by the artillery could not be changed. All battles of the most recent times make it clear that only tanks would have made a real difference."

No information on the effects of this decision on the armaments, equipment, and tactics of the armored artillery is extant. Changes no longer came about, as the war soon ended.

The observer will find a noteworthy agreement if he compares the development of light field guns with that of heavy

In March 1942 the requirements for a light howitzer for the Army were defined anew. They were to weigh less but have the same ballistic performance. To simplify production, the use of a slightly modified mount of the 7.5 cm Antitank Cannon 40 was foreseen. The gun was accepted and designated the 10.5 cm Light Howitzer 18/40; it reached the troops in Spring 1943.

Training on the 10.5 cm Light Howitzer 18 M in the Army Reserve, as seen in the spring of 1944. The replacement personnel for the armored artillery came from reserve and training units of the artillery, while the command personnel were trained in special instructional courses at the artillery schools.

Limited numbers of the 7.5 cm Cannon 7 M 85 reached the troops in 1944. They were a compromise that included the hope of improving the field artillery's ability to defend against tanks. The barrel, cradle with recoil brake, and recuperator of the 7.5 cm Antitank Cannon 40 were mounted on the mount of the 10.5 cm Light Howitzer 18/40. The gun weighed 1778 kg and had a range of 10,275 meters.

howitzers and cannons. The 15 cm Heavy Howitzer 18 had proved to be a very useful gun for the troops. In the motorized armored artillery its high weight of 6304 kilograms played a subordinate role. A major weakness was its short range (13,325 meters), especially opposed to the 17,300 meters of the Russian 152 mm Cannon Howitzer 37.

In May 1942 a new heavy howitzer with ranges up to 17,000 meters had already been called for. There came the 15 cm Heavy Howitzer 42 (ex-18/40) with a range of 15,000 meters. After 46 guns were produced the contract was canceled in the summer of 1942. By the war's end, only mooden mockups of the 15 cm Heavy Howitzer 43, a gun on a three-spar mount, had been built. A range of 18,000 meters was projected.

The steadily decreasing use of the empty Cartridge Case 6350 in the 15 cm Heavy Howitzer 28 inspired wishes to be independent of them and introduce ammunition without metal cases. This war experience led to several new developments for divisional and army artillery being contracted for in 1943. None of these designs was put to use; some existed only on the drawing board. One was the 15.5 cm Heavy Howitzer 44 with a planned range of 18,000 meters. The 12.8 cm Heavy Cannon 44 (range 23,000 meters), which Hitler had promoted in mid-May 1942 to replace the 10 cm Heavy Cannon 18, was still intended for metal cases. Some 25 to 30 barrels were fitted to captured Russian mounts in December 1944 and used in the Ardennes offensive. That was the end of new designs for heavy field guns. In terms of their performance capability, the guns introduced in the armored artillery to the end of the war no longer lived up to the requirements. The troops had to make due with them.

Among the further problems that lessened the effectiveness of the divisional artillery, and thus also the armored artillery during the course of the war, was the increasing shortage of ammunition. In 1941-42 a monthly average of 1,313,287 explosive and hollow-charge shells for the 10.5 cm Light Howitzer 18 had been consumed. For the 15 cm heavy howitzers and 10 cm Heavy Cannon 18 the consumption was 375,080 and 100,606 rounds. In 1942-43 the ammunition consumption of all guns, except the 10 cm Heavy Cannon 18, decreased slightly, but in 1943-44 it increased to almost double the 1941-42 consumption: 2,152,300 rounds by the 10.5 cm light howitzers; 630,200 by the 15 cm heavy howitzers; and 18,000 by the 10 cm heavy cannons. As in the winter of 1941-42, the cases of ammunition shortage increased. For example, the Commander of the 2nd Army (Army Group Center) reported on July 28, 1943, that the ammunition for the 10.5 cm Light Howitzer 18 "was among the short ammunition and thus to be conserved." In the history of Armored Artillery Regiment 103 (4th Armored Division) it is noted repeatedly that this unit's actions suffered from a lack of ammunition. Speer noted during the armament conference with Hitler on October 14-15, 1943:

"The threatening situation with light howitzer ammunition requires immediate production of at least three million rounds and, by December, the increase to four million rounds."

The situation did not improve, but rather grew considerably worse until early 1945. A notice from the General Quartermaster

Russian divisional howitzers also saw service in the armored and armored grenadier divisions in 1943-44. In Armored Artillery Regiment 91 (25th Armored Division) there were three batteries of them, and in the Artillery Regiment (mot.) of the 20th Armored Grenadier Division, one battery. Ammunition was even manufactured for the 12.2 cm Heavy Howitzer 396 (r)-russ-38 from April 1943 on. In 1944, 690,600 rounds were fired.

In the summer of 1944, at the beginning of the fighting in Normandy, the III. Unit of Armored Artillery Regiment 130 (Armored Instructional Division) had twelve 15.2 cm Cannon Howitzer 433/1 (r)-russ.-37-. In marching order the gun weighed 7930 kilograms. The explosive shells weighed 43.5 kg and could be fired up to 17,260 meters.

Light Howitzer Battery (up to 6 guns) (mot.Z.)
War Budget 44, as per War Strength Report No. 450 of June 1, 1944

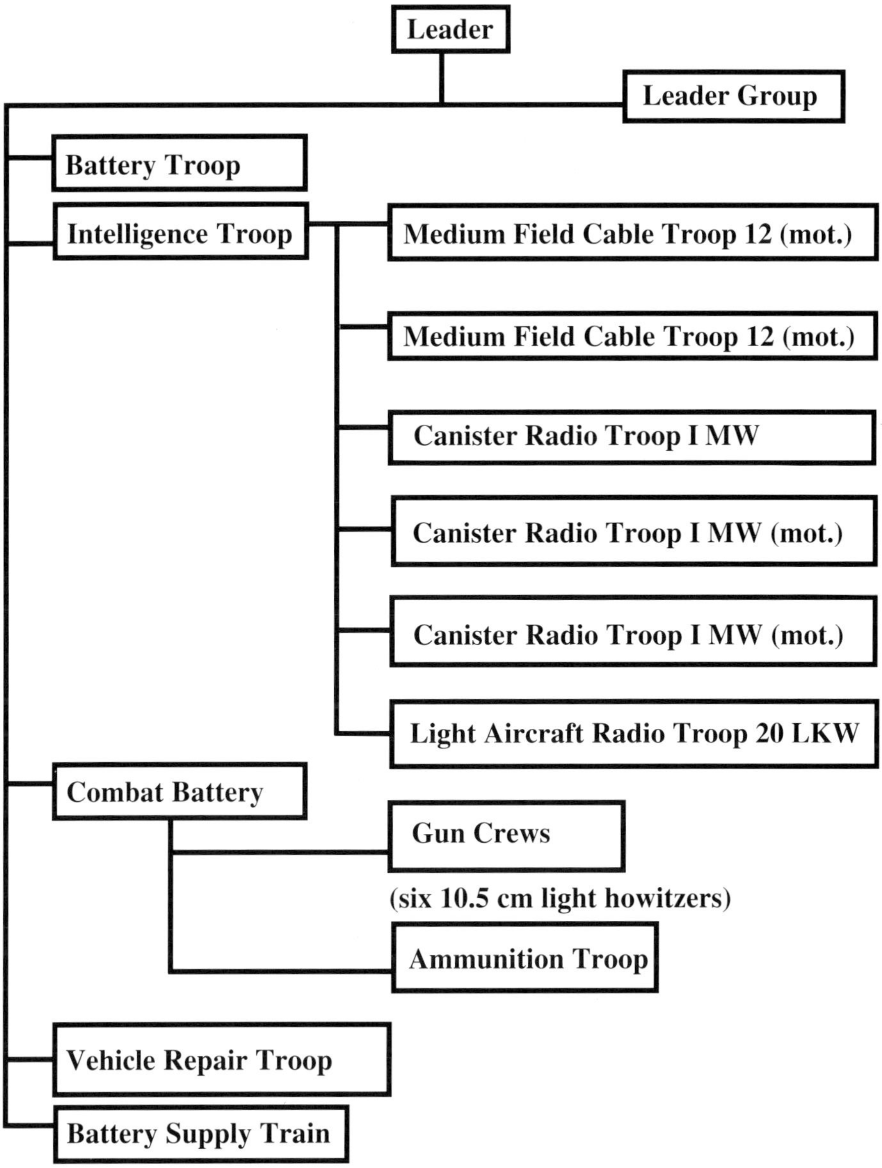

Strength
3/28/85
1 Motorcycle
1 Tracked Cycle (Sd.Kfz.2)
20 Cars and Trucks
6 Light Tractors (Sd.Kfz.11)

Of the 676 delivered 10.5 cm Light Howitzer 18/2 (Sfl.) on Gun Car II "Wespe" (Sd.Kfz.124), 301 were still with the field army in March 1945. Six armored howitzers of this type were with the replacement army. Besides the armored artillery regiments (mot.) of the armored grenadier divisions, a few artillery regiments (mot.) in the armored grenadier divisions had two, or in a few cases three light armored howitzer batteries.

Early in 1945 there were still 335 15 cm Heavy Howitzer 18/1 (Sfl.) on Gun Car III/IV "Hummel" (Sd/.Kfz.165) in the field army, most of them seeing service in the armored divisions on the eastern front.

At the end of 1943 the Army General Staff reported that during a ten-day major attack by the Red Army, 595 shells per 10.5 cm light howitzer were fired. (a weight of some nine tons). Per 15 cm Heavy Howitzer 18 287 shots were fired (= 12.45 tons). The numerous ammunition crates were collected and reused.

Members of the armored artillery stand in front of a 10.5 cm Light Howitzer 18/2 (Sfl.) on Gun Car II "Wespe" (Sd.Kfz.124). From September 15, 1944, on the replacement unit for personnel of the armored howitzer units was the Armored Howitzer Replacement and Training Unit 201 at the Gross-Born training site, Nord-Linde Camp.

Heavy howitzers of the III. (heavy) Unit of an artillery regiment (mot.) in firing position. The basic structure of Armored Grenadier Division 1944 on August 20, 1944, was to include twelve guns of this type. There were also four 10 cm Heavy Cannon 18 and 36 10.5 cm Light Howitzer 18.

Department of the Army General Staff about the Army's ammunition situation, dated January 14, 1945, gives this information:

"The change in ammunition production in the first quarter of 1945, compared to the autumn of 1944, shows for the main types:
Light Howitzer 18, 21% less,
Heavy Howitzer 18, 22% less,
total ammunition 30% less."

For every 10.5 cm Light Howitzer 18, 335 rounds were available; for the 15 cm Heavy Howitzer 18 175 rounds; for the 12.2 cm Heavy Howitzer 396 (r)-russ.38- 165 rounds; and for the 10 cm Heavy Cannon 18, 120 rounds. The conclusions of the General Quartermaster Department seem logical:

"Whether the Army can fulfill the tasks given it in 1945 depends extensively on enemy behavior. Simultaneous major battles on all fronts cannot be supplied with sufficient ammunition and must lead to catastrophe." Nothing needs to be added to that.

Now we come to a further problem of material supplies that particularly affected the mobility of the motorized units of the armored artillery regiments—the degree of their equipping with towing tractors. Important for the armored artillery were—as towing vehicles for the 10.5 cm Light Howitzer 18 and its variants—the 3-ton Light Tractor (Sd.Kfz.11) and the 5-ton Medium Tractor (Sd.Kfz.6). The 8-ton Medium Tractor (Sd.Kfz.7) was used to tow the 15 cm Heavy Howitzer 18 and the 10 cm Heavy Cannon. In January 1942 there were 4182 3-ton tractors, 2592 5-ton, and 3282 8-ton tractors on hand. The yearly production for 1943 was listed at 2153 3-ton, 563 5-ton, and 3251 8-ton tractors. The figures for 1944 followed a similar order, except for the 3-ton Light Tractor (Sd.Kfz.11), of which only 1308 were delivered. Despite the considerable numbers, the motorized units of the armored artillery regiments suffered from an almost chronic shortage of towing vehicles. That had a bad effect on their mobility, and did not correspond to the specific qualities of fast and mobile combat for the armored divisions. In Armored Artillery Regiment 89 (24th Armored Division) on April 1, 1944, five 15 cm

In the autumn of 1943, Artillery Regiment 33 (15th Armored Grenadier Division) had three batteries of light howitzers towed by the Tracked Tractor East.

In 1944 the flak platoons of staff batteries in the artillery regiments (mot.) and armored artillery regiments each had three 2 cm Mountain AA-Gun 38.

Training on the 15 cm Heavy Howitzer 18 (mot.).

armored howitzers, seven 15 cm Heavy Howitzer 18 (mot.Z.), and four 10 cm Heavy Cannon 18 were not ready for use for lack of towing tractors. The 4th Battery of Armored Artillery Regiment 89 had five 10.5 cm light howitzers on that day, but only one towing tractor. Some units were given 2-ton halftrack trucks (Sd.Kfz.3) as temporary towing vehicles in place of the lacking 3-ton light tractors (Sd.Kfz.11). In the 15th Armored Grenadier Division, some batteries of Artillery Regiment (motr.) 33 were even issued Tracked Tractor East (R.S.O.) as towing tractors for their light howitzers. Great efforts were made to raise the numbers of combat-ready towing vehicles, partly by increasing new production, partly through repairs. At the beginning of August 1944 it was decided to increase the monthly production of 1565 towing vehicles of all size classes to 2270 by that December. A further possibility of increasing the field army's supplies was seen in the preparation of repaired vehicles. At the armament conference of September 21-23, 1944, the following decisions were made:

"The 1500 1-ton to 18-ton towing vehicles in the German space that need repairs must be totally overhauled and delivered to the troops ready for action through a forced action no later than October

The basic structure of an armored artillery regiment of an armored division in 1944 included twelve 10.5 cm Light Howitzer 18/2 (Sfl.) on Gun Car II "Wespe" (Sd.Kfz.124), as well as four Gun Car II (Mun.).

In the foreground is a camouflaged "Wespe" armored howitzer; in the background self-propelled guns of the heavy armored howitzer battery have arrived.

In 1942 there were 48 of the 10.5 cm Heavy Howitzer 18 (Sfl.) on Gun Car 39 H (f) produced. This picture shows a self-propelled gun of this type during the fighting in Normandy in July 1944.

The "Hummel" armored howitzer could reach a top speed of 42 kph. Its range was stated as 215 kilometers.

This picture was taken on the eastern front in the spring of 1944. Numerous armored howitzers were no longer ready for service at that time because of technical damage and for lack of suitable towing vehicles.

The barrel of this 15 cm Heavy Howitzer 18/1 (Sfl.) on Gun Car III/IV "Hummel" (Sd/Kfz.165) shows gunshot damage.

15, 1944. Similarly to what is done in the simultaneous tank repair action by dismantling the especially badly damaged vehicles, a reduction of the total number of up to 1000 vehicles can be undertaken if the possibility thereby exists of making these vehicles fully capable for front-line use in a correspondingly short time."

The fact that such special action could not achieve any significant improvement of the situation in the armored artillery regiments is seen in the attack operation "Watch on the Rhine" in the Ardennes in December 1944. Only some 50% of the guns could be made mobile by towing vehicles, sometimes by using the "Maultier" ("Mule," 2-ton halftrack truck). Similar cuts in the size order had to be made in the motor vehicle equipment of the staffs and ammunition units. Fuel shortages also contributed to limiting the mobility of the motorized and armored artillery further. At times it ranked below the level of the horsedrawn artillery in the infantry divisions.

The material situation of the armored artillery influenced its combat value very decisively, but also affected its structure. Before this problem will be depicted in conclusion, it seems appropriate to indicate details in the structure and material equipping of several units. A few examples: The Armored Artillery Instructional Regiment (Armored Artillery Regiment 130) of the [p. 149] Armored Instructional Division established in the soring of 1944 had in its I. Unit three batteries of 10.5 cm light howitzers, in its II. Unit two batteries of 10.5 cm armored howitzers and one battery of 15 cm armored howitzers, and in its III. Unit three batteries of 15.2 cm Cannon Howitzer 433/1(r) russ.37. The twelve guns were something special. With them, targets at distances up to 17,260 meters could be fired on. To be sure, there were no double fuzes for the ammunition, and no foglaying

This picture from the spring of 1944 shows Generalleutnalt Hasso von Manteuffel, Commander of the "Grossdeutschland" Armored Grenadier Division. The "Grossdeutschland" Armored Artillery Regiment had an armored howitzer unit, to which the Armored Scout Car III (Sd.Kfz.143) belonged. According to war strength reports, an armored artillery regiment was to have five armored scout cars and four medium Schützenpanzerwagen.

shells, so that fulfilling typical firing tasks of the armored artillery was only possible within limits. For the guns, which weighed 7130 kg in firing position, 12-ton heavy tractors (Sd/Kfz.8) were needed. In their place were 8-ton medium tractors (Sd.Kfz.7). Their towing power was not sufficient. At St. Lo in France, Armored Artillery Regiment 130 lost almost all its guns. After new supplying in the autumn of 1944, it had the usual equipment, though the light batteries had six 10.5 cm Light Howitzer 18 (mot.Z.). The Armored Artillery Regiment of the "Grossdeutschland" Armored Grenadier Division was also made of four units until its IV. Unit was transferred. In 1944 the IV. Unit became the I. Unit of Corps Asrmored Artillery Regiment 500 of the "Grossdeutschland" Armored Corps. Armored grenadier divisions generally had no units with self-propelled guns. Exceptions were the "Grossdeutschland" Armored Grenadier Division, the 3rd Armored Grenadier Division and the 29th Armored Grenadier Division (one unit each) and the 90th Armored Grenadier Division (two self-propelled batteries). Considerable variations from the Army's basic structure of armored grenadier units existed in the armored or armored grenadier divisions of the Waffen-SS. They had four units.

One unit or individual batteries would be equipped with 17 cm cannons on mortar mounts and with 21 cm Mortar 18 (Army artillery guns). There were also foglaying units or batteries. These troops left the division units with the establishment of the SS Armored Corps in 1944. The structure and equipment of the SS [p. 150] armored artillery paralleled the prevailing Army structure as much as possible till the war ended.

Some armored artillery regiments were equipped with 15 cm foglaying batteries. The 15 cm Foglayer 41 could fire a salvo of six 35.7-kg shells (explosive) or (fog) 6900 meters.

By the end of the war some armored artillery regiments had also received 3.7 cm AA Cannon 43. In marching order the gun weighed 2059 kg. Air targets at altitudes up to 3500 meters could be fired on with hope of success. The range for ground targets was 6500 meters.

On August 3, 1944 a new basic structure was introduced for the armored artillery regiments of the armored divisions, and on August 20, 1944 for the artillery regiments (mot.) of the armored grenadier divisions. The individual divisions were thus equipped with guns as shown:

	Armored Division 44	Armored Grenadier Division 44
10.5 cm armored howitzer	12	—
15 cm armored howitzer	6	—
10.5 cm light howitzer	12	36
15 cm heavy howitzer	8	12
10 cm heavy cannon	4	4
Total	42	52

The most drastic change was that of the batteries to six guns instead of the formerly usual four. This decision was dictated by the concern for sparing materials and personnel. In the History of Armored Artillery Regiment 103 (4th Armored Division) it is stated: "On October 2 the 2nd Battery must be disbanded, as was already ordered on Septemner 8 but not done. It is incredible that for the sake of a very doubtful vehicle saving, an old experienced battery is torn apart. The enemy aerial dominance does not favor the six-gun battery either, as it is now formed."

The light Flak platoons in the staff batteries took over most of the protection from air attacks; in the armored artillery and artillery (mot.) regiments they were equipped with three 2 cm Mountain AA Gun 38 on open 2-ton trucks (War Strength Report No. 585 and 405 (fG). In the armored artillery regiments of the Waffen-SS there were sometimes V. Units, special Flak units with assorted guns. These units had one battery of four 8.8 cm AA Cannon 36 or 37, one battery with nine 3.7 cm AA Cannon 36 (Sfl.)(Sd.Kfz.6/2 or 7/2), one battery of eight 2 cm AA Cannon 38 (Sfl.)(Sd.Kfz.20/5) and two 2 cm Flak Quads (Sfl.)(Sd.Kfz.7/1).

They had a considerably higher firepower and offered better possibilities for defense from low-flying aircraft, even when they handled all the anti-aircraft defense in the whole division sector. The Flak units were later removed from the armored artillery regiments and subordinated directly to the division commanders.

Asccording to Message No. 1/1600/45 gKdos from the Inspector-General of the Armored Troops on March 25, 1945, the accepted structure of Armored Division 45 was mentioned as equaling those of armored divisions and armored artillery regiments. The armored artillery regiments kept their basic structure. Shortages and makeshift means were to make the Inspector-General's instructions easier. Often the armored howitzers of the I. (self-propelled) Units were lacking. Here there had already been major gaps in December 1944. For the "Müncheberg" Armored Division, established on the eastern front early in March 1945, [p. 154] the structure of Armored Division 44 served as a basis. Only a torso of the armored artillery regiment still remained. Accorsing to a message from the chief of the General Staff to the Army High Command on March 14, 1945 (No.1 c/No.3101/45 geh.), the I. Unit was to be assigned three batteries, each with six 10.5 cm Light Howitzer 18/40. They came

To arm the Flak units that were briefly included in the armored artillery regiments, there were 2 cm Flak Quad 38 (Sfl.) on medium tractors (Sd.Kfz.7/1) and . . .

. . . the 3.7 cm Flak Cannon 36. The gun, mounted on Special Trailer 52 (1-axle), weighed 2400 kg in marching trim. Aerial targets could be fired on at altitudes up to 3500 meters.

The heavy batteries of the Flak units were equipped with the 8.8 cm Flak Cannon 36 or 37. With it, aerial targets at heights up to 10,000 meters could be fired on. The great range for ground targets (14,860 meters) was sometimes used to carry out artillery tasks of the armored artillery. The gun was of particular use in antitank defense.

Armored Artillery Regiment 76
at the beginning of 1945

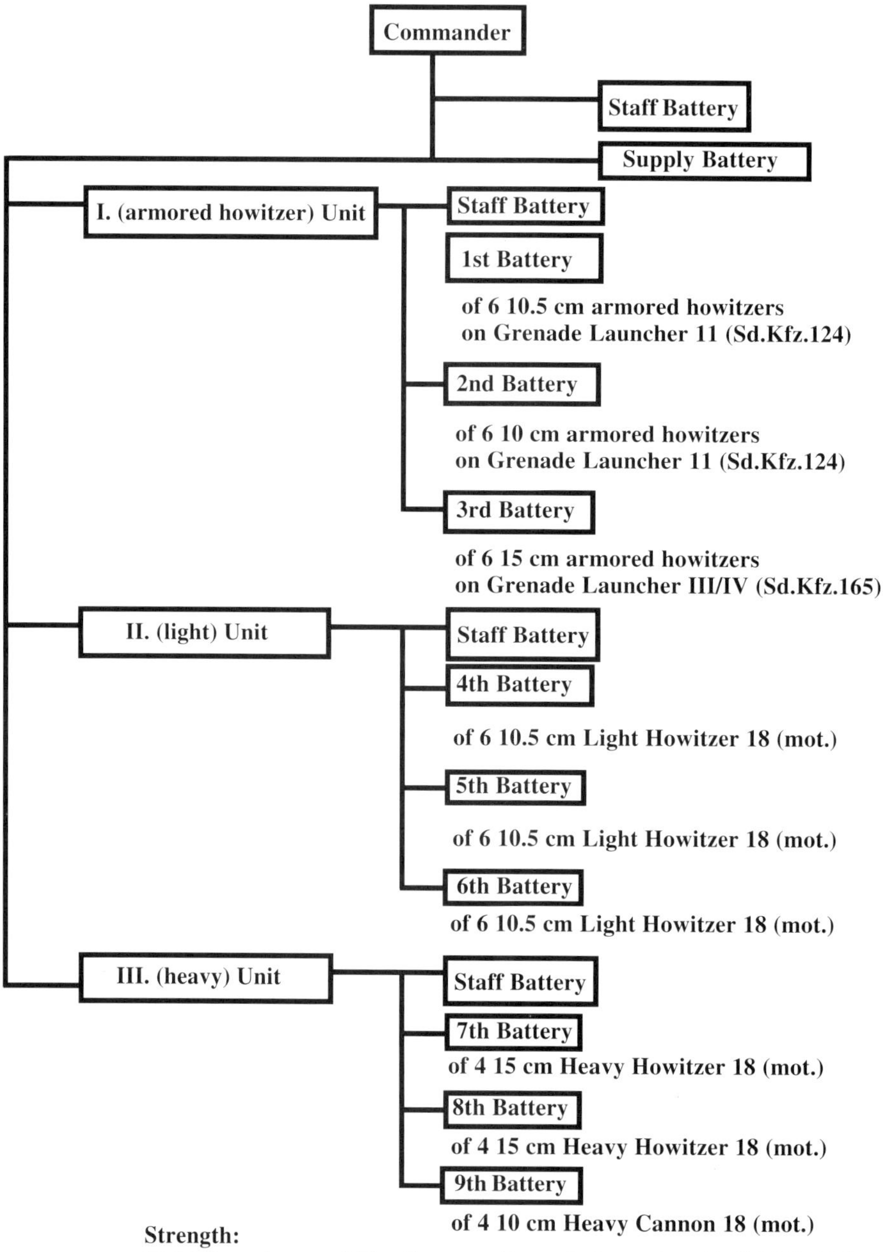

Strength:
12 10.5 cm Armored Howitzers on Grenade Launcher 11 (Sd.Kfz.124)
6 15 cm Armored Howitzer on Grenade Launcher III/IV (Sd.Kfz.165)
18 10.5 cm Light Howitzer 18 (mot.)
8 15 cm Heavy Howitzer 18 (mot.)
4 10 cm Cannon 18 (mot.)

The 10,5 cm Light Howitzer 18/2 (Sfl.) on Gun Car II "Wespe" (Sd.Kfz.124) of the "Hermann Go"ring" Armored Artillery Regiment, which belonged to the "Hermann Go"ring" Paratroop Armored Division of the Luftwaffe. The photos date from the autumn of 1944.

At the end of April 1945, members of the "Hermann Go"ring" Paratroop Armored Division fought in eastern Saxony. The last armored vehicles, including armored howitzers of the Armored Artillery Regiment, had to be abandoned during the withdrawal over the Erzgebirge.

from People's Artillery Corps 411. The II. Unit had one battery with two 2 cm Flak Cannon 38 and four 3.7 cm Flak Cannon 43; the other two batteries each had two 2 cm guns and four 8.8 cm Flak Cannon 36 or 37.

The only advantage of the 8.8 cm guns was that their shells were fired with a higher initial velocity. That improved their potential for antitank use and provided a longer range. For the Führer Escort Brigade, another

Special demands were placed on the crews of armored howitzers. Thus in July 1944 the rank of "Higher Officer for Armored Artillery" was introduced.

armored unit that was being planned early in 1945, the II. Unit of Artillery Instructional Regiment (mot.) 5 of Gross-Born was transferred. It had two batteries of six 10.5 cm Light Howitzer 18/40 (mot.Z.) each, and one battery of four 15 cm Heavy Howitzer 18 (mot.Z.).

In March 1945 the 16th Armored Division was restructured, including the "Jüterbog" Armored Division. Armored Artillery Regiment 16 had two light artillery units and one Flak unit. The I. Unit, Armored Artillery Regiment 16, was the former Artillery Unit 510. It had 16 10.5 cm light howitzers. The II. Unit of Armored Artillery Regiment 16 was composed of the personnel and material that remained of the Armored Artillery Regiment; on February 26, 1945 it had 13 10.5 cm light howitzers. The III. Unit came from the Luftwaffe and was equipped with twelve 8.8 cm Flak Cannon 36 or 37 and six light AA guns. In addition, the 16th Armored Division included Army Flak Artillery Unit 274, but it possessed only light AA guns, including some quads.

The few examples cited here illustrate the decline of the armored artillery in the last weeks of World War II. What remains inthe fact that the structure, armament and equipment, as well as the operational basis, of the armored artillery in the German Army developed to a qualitatively high niveau up to 1943 by depending closely on the development of theoretical and practical principles for the use of large armored troops. The experience thus gained was exemplary and influential for the development of armored artillery units after World War II.

According to the War Strength Report of the armored artillery regiments of the armored divisions in 1944, such units had 55 medium off-road-capable trucks. Here an Opel Blitz 3-ton truck is shown.

In the summer of 1944, production of the 15 cm Heavy Howitzer 18/1 (Sfl.) on Gun Car III/IV "Hummel" had already been halted. The losses on the eastern front are listed as 129 self-propelled mounts from the beginning of July to the end of November 1944. In the west, 29 heavy armored howitzers were lost between September 1 and November 30, 1944.

The self-propelled gun "Lotti" of the 3rd (heavy) Bettery of Armored Artillery Regiment 13 (13th Armored Division) has a kill marked on its barrel. The regiment was wiped out in the Ukraine in August 1944. In November of that year it was reestablished, and in March 1945 it was renamed Armored Artillery Regiment 2 "Feldherrnhalle".

This 15 cm Heavy Howitzer 18/1 (Sfl.) on Gun Car III/IV "Hummel" (Sd.Kfz.165) is a display piece at the Munster Armored Museum. The picture was taken in the mid-nineties during a display of historic military technology.

At the end of January 1944 the decision was made to increase production of the 8.8 cm Tank Destroyer Cannon 43 as soon as possible. It was also decided to use the gun in the artillery. Thus two batteries of Artillery Regiment (mot.) 25 of the 25th Armored Grenadier Division were equipped with this gun. The picture shows the 8.8 cm Tank Destroyer Cannon 43/41, last produced in July 1944.

The artillery power of armored units suffered at the end of 1944 from a lack of fuel and ammunition and the low numbers of usable guns. tractors and self-propelled mounts. The western army reported on December 10, 1944 that it had twenty 15 cm armored howitzers (it should have had 36), seven of which were ready for action. The situation with 10.5 cm armored howitzers was even worse. Out of 72 specified guns it had only fifteen, four of which were ready for action.

A 10.5 cm Light Howitzer 18 M (mot.) in a dug-out firing position (gun cut). More and more often, the lask of towing tractors necessitated using guns of the motorized and armored artillery regiments in fixed positions. Others were made partially mobile with the few available towing vehicles.

In the first two months of 1945 the German forces lost 936 light and 365 heavy howitzers. About 650 and 250 of these guns were produced then. The heavy losses could not be replaced.

An abandoned 8-ton Medium Towing Tractor KM m 11 (Sd.Kfz.7). The Armored Artillery Regiment (free structure) of Armored Division 1944 should have had 15 3-ton light tractors (Sd.Kfz.11) and twelve 8-ton medium tractors (Sd.Kfz.7). Often only a fraction of them were ready for action.

One of the few 3-ton Light Towing Tractor HL kl 6 (Sd.Kfz.11) that survived to the end of the war in 1945. In the eighties it belonged to the Bra"uer vehicle collection in Lengefeld in the Erzgebirge.
[only publisher's name and ISBN on back cover. End of Motart04 file and book.]